M000300921

The Latin Psalter

Introduction, Selected Text and Commentary

David J. Ladouceur

Bristol Classical Press

First published in 2005 by
Bristol Classical Press
an imprint of
Gerald Duckworth & Co. Ltd.
90-93 Cowcross Street, London EC1M 6BF
Tel: 020 7490 7300
Fax: 020 7490 0080
inquiries@duckworth-publishers.co.uk
www.ducknet.co.uk

A catalogue record for this book is available
from the British Library

ISBN 1 85399 683 1

Printed and bound in Great Britain by
Antony Rowe Ltd

Contents

Patri meo sine quo non

Introduction

The importance of the Psalms

To Athanasius, a Christian bishop of the fourth century, the Psalter contained 'the perfect image for the soul's course of life'. Even in the early days of Christianity, the Psalms had their role. To the first Jewish Christians, brought up in the temple services, many Psalms would have been familiar. The New Testament, moreover, cites no book of the Old Testament more often than this so-called 'Bible within the Bible'. Of some 1520 Old Testament citations, over 320 are drawn from the Psalms. If one considers too how the Psalms sometimes implicitly structure gospel narrative, in the Passion account, for example, their significance becomes undeniable. As early as the second century, evidence exists from the Church father Tertullian (*c.* 160-225) that the Psalter was used in the liturgy of the Word. This liturgy focused on scriptural readings for those preparing for baptism. In their Latin form, the Psalms came to assume an oracular function and, to some exegetes, became virtual records of conversation between God, Christ and the Church.

The first Latin translations

Precisely where and when the first Latin translations of the Bible appeared is unknown. Among the answers scholars have given are Syrian Antioch, Rome, and North Africa. The last is the most probable and a date of the late second century similarly likely. In Tertullian there are some ambiguous indications for the use of one or more Latin versions, but it is in Cyprian, bishop of Carthage (d. 258) that the clearest evidence for an authoritative and subsequently influential version occurs.

Why these Latin translations were made is more easily ascertainable. Three centuries before Christ, the Hellenistic Jews of the Diaspora, distanced from their cultural center, had gradually felt the need for a Greek translation of their Hebrew scriptures; hence the origin of that heterogeneous assemblage known as the Septuagint. By no means a linguistic unity, its translations range from literal to free and date perhaps from the third to the second centuries BC. The Psalms may have been translated into Greek in Palestine in the second century BC, though certainty here is impossible. To the early Christians the Septuagint was, according to one tradition, a sacred text whose very translation had been divinely inspired. But in the Roman period, as Latin, in its turn, gradually replaced Greek, the need for Latin translations became acute.

The textual tradition

The textual tradition of the Old Latin Bible translations from the second to the fourth century, collectively called *Vetus Latina*, is complex and no longer entirely recoverable. Some scholars believe that there originally existed a single version which later split into a variety of text forms; others, that variety existed in the beginning and that imperfect attempts at standardization came later. Regardless of the view adopted, certainly early on, provisional versions for local usage must have existed, and there must have been incessant copying, interpolating and glossing. As a result, by the fourth century a state of textual confusion reigned.

The need for standardization

It was, however, at this time that the need for standardization became pressing. Two centuries earlier the Great Church had steered a middle course between Judaizing and Gnosticizing Christianities. To endorse its position, the Church's representatives had turned to the Old Testament for proof-texts. Against the Marcionites they argued for the retention of the Old Testament but only if, as they argued against extreme Judaizers, the texts were interpreted through a new Christological perspective. Hence flourished forms of interpretation – predictive, allegorical, typological – which viewed the Old Testament and, later, especially the Psalter, as witnesses of Christ. By the fourth century, as challenges from Jews and heretics intensified, the need to base interpretations on a solid authoritative text became obvious. In this period there arose, as well, sentiment for liturgical standardization, though local practice in the Eucharistic liturgy, for example, would remain varied for some time thereafter. An obvious prerequisite for standardization was a commonly accepted sacred text.

Jerome and the three versions of the Psalter

Into this confusion came Jerome who, with his usual tendency to exaggeration, asserted that there were as many text forms as there were copies. Already a well known scholar, about 382 he was commissioned by Pope Damasus to produce a standard version of the Gospels. While he was engaged in this official project, he also began work on the Psalter.

Three versions of the Psalter are linked to his name. The first, made at Rome, was, by his own admission, a superficial correction and reworking of the Old Latin text which he based on the best available western text of the Septuagint. Adopted at Rome and used until the sixteenth century, this version was once identified with the so-called Roman Psalter employed at St. Peter's, but since the 1930s this identification has been questioned. A second version was the Gallican Psalter, so-named from its adoption in Gaul in the sixth century perhaps under the influence of Gregory of Tours. This Jerome finished in Bethlehem about 392 after the death of Damasus. It became through the efforts of Alcuin, the religious advisor to Charlemagne, the standard text of the Vulgate. Afterwards, Jerome made a third version, the *Psalterium iuxta Hebraeos*. Directly translated from the Hebrew, it is an accurate and idiomatic translation, but was not in the end fully embraced since its adoption seemed to entail rejection of the divine inspiration of the Septuagint. Also influential was the conservative attitude of an active laity who cherished older translations. Their less informed modern counterparts are those who contend that if the King James version was good enough for St. Paul, it should be good enough for them.

The Gallican Psalter

Since the Gallican Psalter is the subject of this commentary, a few words of characterization are in order. It may be succinctly described as an *emendatio* of a *translatio*, i.e. a correction of a translation, specifically the Old Latin translation which had been based on a western form of the Septuagint. In the East, Jerome had access to the elaborate edition of the Old Testament drawn up by Origen and known as the Hexapla. For most of the Old Testament it contained six columns: a Hebrew text, a Hebrew text transliterated into Greek letters, and four other Greek versions including a revised Septuagint.

The Hexaplaric Septuagint was textually superior to the western version. It thus allowed Jerome, like Origen, to signal with obelus and asterisk, the symbols of Homeric textual scholarship, the differences between itself and the Hebrew. Though it did have a corrective influence, again conservative attitudes limited the changes that Jerome could make. Also, he was still not, in general, working directly from the Hebrew but from the Greek. What problems existed in the Greek, therefore, were often carried over into the Latin text. Unless influenced by theological and social preconceptions, the Septuagint translators, for example, often used formal equivalents for the Hebrew perfective and imperfective 'tenses'. They thus levelled and sometimes misrepresented many subtle and complex verbal uses that are independent of time distinctions. This crude translation *ad verbum* in place of *ad sensum* is then adopted into the Latin text. As a result, the modern translator of the Latin text confronts at times seemingly unidiomatic uses and shifts of tenses within a Psalm. To ancient and medieval exegetes, however, these linguistic puzzles offered opportunities to discover Christological or eschatological references. Calques, verbatim translations of the Hebrew into Greek, which are then taken over into Latin, also produce obscurities.

The Latin of the Psalms is also influenced by Greek. Greek words are sometimes merely transliterated. Syntactical structures are taken over, e.g. the substantive participle in the oblique cases used frequently in place of a relative clause. To complicate the matter, one must also reckon with the long linguistic interaction between Greek and Latin in the higher as well as lower classes of society. As a result, modern scholarship perhaps too positively and neatly categorizes certain phenomena in the Latin text as Hellenisms.

The Latin itself, moreover, is hardly classical idiom but manifests some tendencies of Vulgar Latin and features of the Old Latin of the second century AD. Semantic shifts, the use of syntactical structures found in the so called *sermo plebeius*, all pose difficulties for someone used to the classical idiom. In this connection, Augustine's well-known statement is often quoted, '*Melius est reprehendant grammatici quam non intelligant populi*'. In its actual context, however, in a comment on Psalm 138, he is replacing the Psalm's classical *os*, apparently no longer pronounced with a distinct quantitative '*o*', with vulgar *ossum*. One must, therefore, be wary of overgeneralizing about the complex nature of this Latin. Finally, the special uses and several registers of Christian Latin cannot be totally ignored.

The object of this commentary

This commentary focuses primarily on these linguistic problems. The quality of individual Psalms and their usefulness in illustrating a wide range of grammatical points have dictated their selection. The need for modern commentaries to guide the non-specialist through the difficulties of later Latin texts is obvious. The few rather old Vulgate grammars that exist tend to base many of their observations on the New Testament, which is not completely representative of other Vulgate texts. Also, older commentaries on the Vulgate Psalter tend to force translations based on the Hebrew onto the Latin text and are inclined to isolate the language from its historical milieu.

Apart from linguistic remarks, therefore, here and there in the commentary, exegesis from the Church fathers is drawn in so that the student may see how someone whose idiom was Latin would naturally interpret the text. This approach provides a more historical linguistic analysis compared with those of the older commentaries. In his *Ennarationes in Psalmos*, Augustine is useful to a certain extent precisely because he was deficient in Hebrew and had, by his own perhaps too modest admission, imperfect knowledge of Greek. It must be kept in mind, however, that his text of the Psalms was not identical to the Gallican, though in his later commentaries he was clearly influenced by it. In addition, without some reference to the underlying Hebrew and Greek, it is impossible to understand intelligently this translation of a translation. For the beginner, this material has been translated everywhere and, in the case of the Hebrew, also transliterated.

The introductory nature and Latin linguistic focus of this commentary do dictate some simplifications which will be obvious to the professional scholar but should be stated expressly for the uninitiated. The commentary is not concerned with a sophisticated treatment of problems in textual criticism. The relationships between the Hebrew text (the so-called Massoretic text), the Septuagint, and the Vulgate are complex. Some scholars, for example, believe that a written Septuagint was assembled from numerous oral translations of parts of the text. From this written text later variants arose. Others believe that there was a standard original translation. One should not assume that what is printed in modern editions is identical to what was available to the ancients, especially in the case of the Hebrew. For an introduction to the range of early divergent texts available, including fragmentary Greek biblical manuscripts found in the Judaean Desert and the Qumran material, and their complex relationships, *Invitation to the Septuagint* (Baker Academic, 2000) by Karen H. Jobes and Moises Silva is excellent.

As an additional complicating element, the Hebrew texts of the Septuagint translators were unpointed, i.e. consonantal texts, written without vowels. Depending on many circumstances, divergent interpretations of the same text were sometimes possible. Both the Septuagint and the Vulgate, accordingly, must be viewed not merely as translations but also interpretations, each within its own historical context. In the case of the Psalms, therefore, many have their own histories and even minor details of translation are dependent upon specific context and use even within the same religious tradition.

Though the commentary refers to Vulgate Latin, this must not be thought of as a linguistic unity any more than Septuagintal Greek or Vulgar Latin or Medieval Latin. The term 'Christian' exegesis or interpretation used in the commentary need not be taken as a normative tradition, i.e. one universally agreed to. In general, but especially in the early centuries, Christian exegetes were hardly ever of one mind in their understanding of the Psalms or, for that matter, of anything else in the Old Testament.

A projected more elaborate edition of the Psalms will deal with these problems in detail and cite the exact patristic evidence, both western and eastern. Finally, the analysis of the Psalms from the Hebrew perspective is far more controversial than can be indicated here, and some statements may appear dogmatic. The interpretation and sometimes inadequate categorizing of individual Psalms, the reconstruction of their setting, even such details as how to translate the verbs, have been and still are matters of great controversy among

Hebraists. The bibliography will provide some guidance on these matters.

The commentary is based on a modern standard text, the fourth edition of *Biblia Sacra iuxta Vulgatam Versionem* (Stuttgart, 1994), edited by Robert Weber and others. Weber's text, however, with its lack of punctuation, presents difficulties for beginners. To avoid copyright issues, I have used nineteenth and early twentieth-century sources for the text, with full traditional punctuation and capitalization. These sources are, fortunately, with only a few exceptions, identical to Weber's text. Any deviations from Weber's text are noted in bold in the text itself. In the commentary, the text is cited according to Weber's unpunctuated version. The student should keep in mind that all capitalization and punctuation are in themselves forms of interpretation.

Notes on Hebrew Grammar

The Latin of the Psalter follows closely the Greek of the Septuagintal translations, which, in turn, adheres closely to the Hebrew texts. Such literal translating inevitably produces a foreign cast to a Latin, which also differs clearly, in its historical and social contexts, from the classical literary Latin of Cicero. This outline represents some of the Semitic features of the texts selected for this book.

The noun

Gender

Hebrew has two genders, masculine and feminine, unlike Latin, which also has a neuter gender.

In Hebrew the feminine is used in place of the neuter and sometimes this usage is adopted in the Latin: Ps 26.4: '*unam petii a Domino, hanc requiram,*' 'One thing I have asked from the Lord, this one thing I shall seek.'

Number

The collective singular is common in Hebrew.

The Hebrew plural is used to enumerate countables, but also has other functions.

(1) The plural of a noun is sometimes used to intensify the idea of the singular. This is the so-called **plural of eminence** or **intensifying plural**. The use of the plural Elohim to refer to the God of Israel is one example.
(2) Abstract nouns are used in the plural as if to encompass concrete manifestations of their quality. Thus 'blindness' is expressed by the plural 'blindnesses'

(3) **A plural of composition** emphasizes the breaking apart of the collection. Thus 'blood' in the body is singular, but 'blood that is shed' is plural.

Cases

Although older grammars speak of nominative, genitive, dative and accusative 'cases' in Hebrew, the language, unlike Latin, which is inflected, does not have an elaborate system of inflection, marked by terminations. In forming the equivalent of the Latin noun plus a modifying genitive, Hebrew shortens the pronunciation of the first noun and accents the second half of the expression. This structure is called a **construct chain**, which is exemplified below under the adjective.

Many proper names are treated as indeclinables, although, rather inconsistently, they sometimes are treated as third-declension nouns with endings.

The adjective

Unlike Latin, Hebrew does not have a wealth of adjectives. In Hebrew, a construct chain is sometimes used as a substitute for a noun modified by adjective. Again, the two nouns are linked by shortening the pronunciation of the first noun. In Latin, the first noun is unaltered while the second noun is modified to the genitive; e.g. *vir pacis,* 'a man of peace', 'a peaceful man'.

Comparison

Adjectives in Hebrew are not declined in positive, comparative and superlative degrees. Instead a preposition **'min'** is used thus: 'He is big from (relative to) her.' In Latin this structure is imitated with the prepositions *super* and *ab*.

Relative clauses

In Hebrew the **relative marker** remains unchanged and a resumptive pronoun is added to show how the case relates to the verb: e.g. 'The man RELATIVE MARKER I see him (resumptive pronoun),' 'The man whom I see,' The man RELATIVE MARKER I give the book to him,' 'the man to whom I give the book.' Latin naturally inflects the relative pronoun itself.

Verbs

In Latin the verbs, with few exceptions, are classified into four conjugations. In dictionaries, the second principal part, the present infinitive, clearly marks to what conjugation a verb belongs. There are six tenses in the indicative mode, four in the subjunctive, and two, in regular use, in the imperative. There are two voices: active and passive.

Hebrew classifies verbs by the number of consonants (radicals) found in the dictionary entry. If, for example, a verb has three radicals, it is a triliteral; if, four, a quadriliteral.

A Hebrew verb, in theory, possesses seven so-called conjugations or verbal patterns. These conjugations are better referred to as 'voices' or 'formatives' since what they do is change the relationship of the subject to the verb. While Latin has only two voices, then, Hebrew has seven: (1) the **qal,** which is the simple active (he watched); (2) the **niphal** which is the simple passive (he was watched); (3) the **piel** which is intensive (he watched energetically); (4) the **pual** which intensive passive (he was watched energetically); (5) the **hiphil**, which is causative active (he caused to watch); (6) the **hophal**, which is causative passive (he was caused to watch); (7) the **hithpael**, which is reflexive (he watched himself).

This traditional representation is mechanical and schematic, and in the wake of modern linguistic research, oversimplified. Many verbs do not appear in all seven voices. The function of the individual voices is wider than indicated. The piel, for example, has other functions besides intensification. It is sometimes causative when states rather than actions are involved.

In each of these conjugations, there are two so-called tenses, **perfective** and **imperfective**, also called **perfect** and **imperfect**.

This use of 'tense', which implies time distinctions, is misleading since certain verbs in the perfect may refer to what is completed in past, present, or future time while the imperfect may refer to what is not finished either in present, future, or past time. Modern grammars describe the perfective as referring to an event, the non-perfective as referring to a process.

In the Latin Psalms, there was a mechanical tendency, following the Greek translators, to translate these into simple past or future tenses which produces a number of difficulties. These difficulties then catalyse exegetical solutions. In the notes, these mistranslations have been discussed in detail.

To give some idea of the complexity involved, the perfect may, in fact, represent the simple English past, the present perfect with 'have', the pluperfect with 'had', the present state with verbs expressing a mental state or action just completed, a generalization, a perfect of confidence, where English would use the future perfect. The imperfect, depending on context, may be translated as past, present, or future, and, given its nuance of incompleteness, often is best translated modally; e.g. as a Latin subjunctive ('let him do it').

The following are some common perfects and imperfects found in the Psalms which are often mistranslated:

Perfects: (1) **Perfect of confidence** In the confident imagination of the speaker a future event is conceived as completed. In Latin, the perfect is often used as a literal equivalent instead of the future, a better rendering. The so-called **prophetic perfect**, found in Isaiah, Jeremiah, and the Psalms is essentially the same usage. (2) **Precative perfect** (Perfect of Prayer) The perfect expresses a prayer or wish and is sometimes better translated as an imperative rather than mechanically as a perfect indicative.

Imperfects: (1) **Cohortative imperfect**, urging an action, 'Let me do this.' (2) **Imperfect of permission** The speaker furnishes his permission to the subject to do something, 'He may do this.' (3) **Imperfect of injunction** The speaker expresses his will in the form of a request or command, 'Do this.'

A Hebrew infinitive is used sometimes to intensify a verb of the same root: 'to kill I will kill', 'I will surely kill'. This is the so-called **infinitive absolute** construction.

Glossary of Grammatical Terms

Terms marked **HG** are to be found in the Outline of Hebrew Grammar above.

adhortatory Making a strong assertion or declaration.

articular infinitive In Greek, the infinitive used with the definite article, 'the to do', equal to the English gerund, 'the doing'. One common Septuagintal construction is literally 'In the him to do this', which is close to the Hebrew construction and is best translated in Latin as a cum clause: 'When he was doing this'.

asseverative Making an emphatic declaration or statement.

calque A virtually word-for-word translation.

cohortative A verbal form expressing encouragement, e.g. 'Let us fight'.

cognate accusative A construction in which the verb and the direct object are derived from the same root, e.g. 'I dreamed a dream'.

construct chain HG

crux A textual passage presenting unusual difficulties.

factitive A verbal form expressing the causing of a state. 'They made him king.'

gnomic Expressing general truths or aphorisms.

hiphil HG

imperfect of permission HG

imperfect of injunction HG

infinitive absolute HG

intensifying Hebrew plural HG

lacuna Gap, missing part.

metonymy Use of the name of one object for another, e.g. 'sceptre' for 'sovereignty'.

modal Expressing manner.

perfects of confidence HG

piel HG

plural of composition HG

precative perfect HG

prophetic preterite HG

prosopopoeia Personification

relative marker HG

substantival Functioning like a noun

Tetragrammaton The four-letter Hebrew word for God, YHWH.

vocalization Inserting vowels in pronouncing a script that is consonantal.

volitional Expressing a wish.

Bibliography and Abbreviations

Bibliography

This select bibliography offers only a starting point and, with few exceptions, focuses on works in English. For a recent comprehensive bibliography, Thorne Wittstruck, *The Book of Psalms: An Annotated Bibliography* (New York, 1994).

General studies

For a general orientation to the Psalms, see Klaus Seybold, *Introducing the Psalms* (Edinburgh, 1990). For invaluable historical perspective see William L. Holladay, *The Psalms through Three Thousand Years* (Minneapolis, 1993).

For a recent study of the Latin translations of the Bible and a more detailed bibliography, see Benjamin Kedar, 'The Latin Translations' in Martin Jan Mulder, ed., *Mikra* (Philadelphia, 1988). In French there are several valuable articles in Jacques Fontaine and Charles Pietri, *Le monde latin antique et la Bible* (Paris, 1985), including Colette Estin, 'Les traductions du Psautier.'

The Gallican Psalter

The following older editions, though much in need of revision and written from a practical perspective for seminarians and clergy, remain useful. They incorporate much traditional exegesis, some of which is in Latin and has been consulted, but not referenced in detail in this commentary. Their translations are, however, often harmonizations based on the Hebrew text. Each contains references to still older but valuable bibliography which remains of great use.

T.E. Bird, *Commentary on the Psalms*, 2 vols (London, 1927).
Patrick Boylan, *The Psalms* I (Dublin, 1921), II (Dublin, 1924).

Steenkiste, J.A. van, *Commentarius in librum psalmorum ad usum seminarii et cleri Brugensis*, 3 vols (Bruges, 1846).

For an old and curiously eclectic commentary with some interesting remarks, see J.M. Neale and R.F. Littledale, *A Commentary on the Psalms from Primitive and Medieval Writers*, vols I-IV (London, 1868-1874).

The language of the Psalms and the Vulgate

Franz Kaulen, *Handbuch zur Vulgata* (Freiburg-in-Breisgau, 1904) and its English counterpart W.E. Plater and H.J. White, *A Grammar of the Vulgate* (Oxford, 1926) remain valuable, though again in need of revision.

John J. Jepson, *The Latinity of the Vulgate Psalter*, Diss. (Catholic University of America, 1915) offers some help but covers only a very small sample of the Psalms.

Matthew Britt, ed., *A Dictionary of the Psalter* (New York, 1923) is generally excellent but sometimes forces the text into the Hebrew mould. In general, the older linguistic reference works and commentaries tend to treat Vulgate Latin in isolation from the broader background of later Latin.

Philip Burton, *The Old Latin Gospels* (Oxford, 2000) with extensive updated bibliography.

Commentaries

Among the more useful recent commentaries on the Psalms are:

Peter C. Craigie, *Psalms 1-50*, Word Biblical Commentary, 19 (Waco, 1983).

Marvin E. Tate, *Psalms 51-100*, Word Biblical Commentary, 20 (Waco, 1990).

Leslie C. Allen, *Psalms 101-150*, Word Biblical Commentary, 21 (Waco, 1983).

Hans-Joachim Kraus, *Psalms 1-59, A Commentary*, trans. Hilton C. Oswald (Minneapolis, 1988).

Hans-Joachim Kraus, *Psalms 60-150, A Commentary*, trans. Hilton C. Oswald, Minneapolis, 1989).

A.A. Anderson, *The Book of Psalms*, 2 vols, The New Century Bible Commentary (Grand Rapids, 1972).

Willem A. VanGemeren, 'Psalms' in Frank E. Gaebelein, ed., *The Expositor's Bible Commentary*, vol. 5 (Grand Rapids, 1991).

Amos Hakham, *The Bible Psalms with the Jerusalem Commentary* vols 1-3 (Jerusalem, 2003).

For current online bibliography see
http//www.osb.org/rbbib/psalmi.html.

*

Special thanks are owed to James Adair for his permission to use the SP fonts for Hebrew and Greek in this book. His official Web site is (http://purl.org/TC/fonts).

Abbreviations

V	Vulgate
Jer.	Psalterium iuxta Hebraeos
MT	Massoretic text
LXX	Septuagint
NIV	New International Version
Ps.	Psalm

Pronunciation of Hebrew

For the non-Semitist, a simplified modern Sephardic pronunciation is used here. A Hebrew syllable is either open (ends in a vowel) or closed (ends in a consonant). A syllable generally cannot begin with a vowel.

Consonants

ʾ	silent
b	ban
ḇ	van
g ḡ	god
d ḏ	door
h	house
w	van
z	zebra
ḥ	Bach
ṭ	tall
y	yes
k	king
ḵ	Bach
l	look
m	mother
n	now
s	sun
ʿ	silent
p	pear
p̄	fear
ṣ	rats
q	kitten
r	rob
ś	sun
š	sheet
t ṯ	tall

Vowels

ā a	father
ı i î	bee
ē ê	they
e	bed
o ô	row
u û	pool
ə	e very quickly pronounced
ă	very short a

Table of Psalms

The Vulgate numbering of the Psalms follows the LXX which differs
from the Hebrew. Differences arose because sometimes two Psalms
in the Hebrew were transmitted as one in the Greek; thus Hebrew 9-
10 = Greek 9 (A/B). Also sometimes one Psalm in Hebrew was
transmitted as two in the Greek; e.g. Hebrew 147 = Greek 146-147.

Graeco-Latin	Hebrew	Graeco-Latin	Hebrew
1	1	125	126
2	2	126	127
3	3	127	128
4	4	128	129
5	5	129	130
6	6	130	131
7	7	132	133
8	8	150	150
9 (A/B)	9-10		
10	11		
11	12		
12	13		
13	14		
14	15		
15	16		
18	19		
19	20		
22	23		
23	24		
25	26		
31	32		
37	38		
38	39		
41	42		
42	43		
50	51		
109	110		
119	120		
121	122		
122	123		
123	124		

Latin Text

Psalm 1

1. Beatus vir, qui non abiit in consilio impiorum, et in via peccatorum non stetit, et in cathedra pestilentiae non sedit:

2. Sed in lege Domini voluntas eius, et in lege eius meditabitur die ac nocte.

3. Et erit tamquam lignum, quod plantatum est secus decursus aquarum, quod fructum suum dabit in tempore suo: et folium eius non defluet: et omnia quaecumque faciet prosperabuntur.

4. Non sic impii, non sic: sed tamquam pulvis, quem proicit ventus a facie terrae.

5. Ideo non resurgent impii in iudicio: neque peccatores in consilio iustorum.

6. Quoniam novit Dominus viam iustorum: et iter impiorum peribit.

Psalm 2

Psalmus David

1. Quare fremuerunt gentes, et populi meditati sunt inania?

2. Adstiterunt reges terrae, et principes convenerunt in unum adversus Dominum, adversus Christum eius.

Diapsalma

3. Disrumpamus vincula eorum: et proiciamus a nobis iugum ipsorum.

4. Qui habitat in caelis inridebit eos: et Dominus subsannabit eos.

5. Tunc loquetur ad eos in ira sua, et in furore suo conturbabit eos.

6. Ego autem constitutus sum rex ab eo super Sion montem sanctum eius, praedicans praeceptum eius.

7. Dominus dixit ad me: Filius meus es tu, ego hodie genui te.

8. Postula a me, et dabo tibi gentes hereditatem tuam, et possessionem tuam terminos terrae.

9. Reges eos in virga ferrea, et tamquam vas figuli confringes eos.

10. Et nunc, reges, intelligite: erudimini, qui iudicatis terram.

11. Servite Domino in timore: et exultate ei cum tremore.

12. Adprehendite disciplinam, nequando irascatur Dominus, et pereatis de via iusta.

13. Cum exarserit in brevi ira eius, beati omnes qui confidunt in eo.

Psalm 3

1. Psalmus David, cum fugeret a facie Abessalon filii sui.

2. Domine, quid multiplicati sunt qui tribulant me? Multi insurgunt adversum me.

3. Multi dicunt animae meae: Non est salus ipsi in Deo eius.
Diapsalma

4. Tu autem, Domine, susceptor meus es, gloria mea, et exaltans caput meum.

5. Voce mea ad Dominum clamavi: et exaudivit me de monte sancto suo.
Diapsalma

6. Ego dormivi, et soporatus sum: et exsurrexi, quia Dominus **suscepit** (W, suscipiet) me.

7. Non timebo milia populi circumdantis me: exsurge, Domine, salvum me fac, Deus meus.

8. Quoniam tu percussisti omnes adversantes mihi sine causa: dentes peccatorum contrivisti.

9. Domini est salus: et super populum tuum benedictio tua.

Psalm 4

1. In finem in carminibus, Psalmus David.

2. Cum invocarem exaudivit me Deus iustitiae meae: in tribulatione dilatasti mihi.

Miserere mei, et exaudi orationem meam.

3. Filii hominum usquequo gravi corde? Ut quid diligitis vanitatem, et quaeritis mendacium?

Diapsalma

4. Et scitote quoniam miraficavit Dominus sanctum suum: Dominus exaudiet me cum clamavero ad eum.

5. Irascimini, et nolite peccare: quae dicitis in cordibus vestris, in cubilibus vestris conpungimini.

Diapsalma

6. Sacrificate sacrificium iustitiae, et sperate in Domino. Multi dicunt: Quis **ostendit** (W, ostendet) nobis bona?

7. Signatum est super nos lumen vultus tui Domine: dedisti laetitiam in corde meo.

8. A fructu frumenti et vini et olei sui, multiplicati sunt.

9. In pace in id ipsum dormiam, et requiescam:

10. Quoniam tu, Domine, singulariter in spe constituisti me.

Psalm 5

1. In finem pro ea, quae hereditatem consequitur, Psalmus David.

2. Verba mea auribus percipe, Domine, intellege clamorem meum.

3. Intende voci orationis meae, rex meus et Deus meus.

4. Quoniam ad te orabo: Domine, mane exaudies vocem meam.

5. Mane adstabo tibi et videbo: quoniam non Deus volens iniquitatem tu es.

6. Neque habitabit iuxta te malignus: neque permanebunt iniusti ante oculos tuos.

7. Odisti omnes, qui operantur iniquitatem: perdes omnes, qui loquuntur mendacium. Virum sanguinum et dolosum abominabitur Dominus:

8. ego autem in multitudine misericordiae tuae,

introibo in domum tuam: adorabo ad templum sanctum tuum in timore tuo.

9. Domine, deduc me in iustitia tua: propter inimicos meos dirige in conspectu **tuo** (W, meo) viam meam.

10. Quoniam non est in ore eorum veritas: cor eorum vanum est.

11. Sepulchrum patens est guttur eorum, linguis suis dolose agebant, iudica illos, Deus.

Dedicant a cogitationibus suis, secundum multitudinem impietatum eorum expelle eos, quoniam inritaverunt te, Domine.

12. Et laetentur omnes, qui sperant in te, in aeternum exultabunt: et habitabis in eis.

Et gloriabuntur in te omnes, qui diligunt nomen tuum.

13. quoniam tu benedices iusto.

Domine, ut scuto bonae voluntatis coronasti nos.

Psalm 6

1. In finem in carminibus, pro octava Psalmus David.

2. Domine, ne in furore tuo arguas me, neque in ira tua corripias me.

3. Miserere mei, Domine, quoniam infirmus sum: sana me, Domine, quoniam conturbata sunt ossa mea.

4. Et anima mea turbata est valde: et tu, Domine, usquequo?

5. Convertere, Domine, eripe animam meam: salvum me fac propter misericordiam tuam.

6. Quoniam non est in morte qui memor sit tui: in inferno autem quis confitebitur tibi?

7. Laboravi in gemitu meo lavabo per singulas noctes lectum meum: in lacrimis meis stratum meum rigabo.

8. Turbatus est a furore oculus meus: inveteravi inter omnes inimicos meos.

9. Discedite a me, omnes qui operamini iniquitatem: quoniam exaudivit Dominus vocem fletus mei.

10. Exaudivit Dominus deprecationem meam, Dominus orationem meam suscepit.

11. Erubescant, et conturbentur vehementer omnes inimici mei: convertantur et erubescant valde velociter.

Psalm 7

1. Psalmus David, quem cantavit Domino pro verbis Chusi filii Iemini.

2. Domine Deus meus, in te speravi: salvum me fac ex omnibus persequentibus me, et libera me.

3. Nequando rapiat ut leo animam meam, dum non est qui redimat, neque qui salvum faciat.

4. Domine Deus meus, si feci istud, si est iniquitas in manibus meis:

5. si reddidi retribuentibus mihi mala, decidam merito ab inimicis meis inanis.

6. Persequatur inimicus animam meam, et conprehendat, et conculcet in terra vitam meam, et gloriam meam in pulverem deducat.

Diapsalma

7. Exsurge, Domine, in ira tua: exaltare in finibus inimicorum meorum.

Et exsurge, Domine Deus meus, in praecepto quod mandasti:

8. et synagoga populorum circumdabit te.

Et propter hanc in altum regredere:

9. Dominus iudicat populos.

Iudica me, Domine, secundum iustitiam meam, et secundum innocentiam meam super me.

10. Consummetur nequitia peccatorum et diriges iustum et scrutans corda et renes Deus.

11. Iustum adiutorium meum a **Domino** (W, Deo), qui salvos facit rectos corde.

12. Deus iudex iustus, fortis, et patiens: numquid irascitur per singulos dies?

13. Nisi conversi fueritis, gladium suum vibrabit: arcum suum tetendit et paravit illum.

14. Et in eo paravit vasa mortis, sagittas suas ardentibus effecit.

15. Ecce parturiit iniustitiam: (W, add et) concepit dolorem, et peperit iniquitatem.

16. Lacum aperuit, et effodit eum et **incidit** (W, incidet) in foveam, quam fecit.

17. Convertetur dolor eius in caput eius: et in verticem ipsius iniquitas eius descendet.

18. Confitebor Domino secundum iustitiam eius: et psallam nomini Domini altissimi.

Psalm 8

1. In finem pro torcularibus, Psalmus David.

2. Domine Dominus noster, quam admirabile est nomen tuum in universa terra!

Quoniam elevata est magnificentia tua super caelos.

3. Ex ore infantium et **lactentium** (W, lactantium) perfecisti laudem propter inimicos tuos, ut destruas inimicum et ultorem.

4. Quoniam videbo caelos tuos, opera digitorum tuorum: lunam et stellas, quae tu fundasti.

5. Quid est homo, quod memor es eius? Aut filius hominis, quoniam visitas eum?

6. Minuisti eum paulo minus ab angelis, gloria et honore coronasti eum:

7. Et constituisti eum super opera manuum tuarum.

8. Omnia subiecisti sub pedibus eius, oves et boves universas: insuper et pecora campi.

9. Volucres caeli, et pisces maris, qui perambulant semitas maris.

10. Domine Dominus noster, quam admirabile est nomen tuum in universa terra!

Psalm 9

1. In finem pro occultis filii, Psalmus David.

2. Confitebor tibi, Domine, in toto corde meo: narrabo omnia mirabilia tua.

3. Laetabor et exultabo in te: psallam nomini tuo, Altissime,

4. In convertendo inimicum meum retrorsum: infirmabuntur, et peribunt a facie tua.

5. Quoniam fecisti iudicium meum et causam meam: sedisti super thronum qui iudicas iustitiam.

6. Increpasti gentes, et periit impius: nomen eorum **delesti** (W, delisti) in aeternum, et in saeculum saeculi.

7. Inimici defecerunt frameae in finem: et civitates eorum destruxisti. Periit memoria eorum cum sonitu:

8. Et Dominus in aeternum permanet. Paravit in iudicio thronum suum:

9. Et ipse iudicabit orbem terrae in aequitate, iudicabit populos in iustitia.

10. Et factus est Dominus refugium pauperi: adiutor in oportunitatibus, in tribulatione.

11. Et sperent in te qui noverunt nomen tuum: quoniam non dereliquisti quaerentes te, Domine.

12. Psallite Domino, qui habitat in Sion: adnuntiate inter gentes studia eius:

13. Quoniam requirens sanguinem eorum recordatus est: non est oblitus clamorem pauperum.

14. Miserere mei, Domine: vide humilitatem meam de inimicis meis.

15. Qui exaltas me de portis mortis, ut adnuntiem omnes laudationes tuas in portis filiae Sion.

16. Exultabo in salutari tuo: infixae sunt gentes in interitu, quem fecerunt.

In laqueo isto, quem absconderunt, conprehensus est pes eorum.

17. **Cognoscetur** (W, cognoscitur) Dominus iudicia faciens: in operibus manuum suarum conprehensus est peccator.

Canticum Diapsalmatis

18. Convertantur peccatores in infernum, omnes gentes quae obliviscuntur Deum.

19. Quoniam non in finem oblivio erit pauperis: patientia pauperum non peribit in finem.

20. Exsurge, Domine, non confortetur homo: iudicentur gentes in conspectu tuo.

21. Constitue, Domine, legislatorem super eos: **ut** (W, omit ut) sciant gentes quoniam homines sunt.

Diapsalma

22 (1). Ut quid, Domine, recessisti longe, despicis in oportunitatibus, in tribulatione?

23 (2). Dum superbit impius, incenditur pauper: conprehenduntur in consiliis quibus cogitant.

24 (3). Quoniam laudatur peccator in desideriis animae suae: et iniquus benedicitur.

25 (4). Exacerbavit Dominum peccator, secundum multitudinem irae suae non quaeret.

26 (5). Non est Deus in conspectu eius: inquinatae sunt viae illius in omni tempore. Auferuntur iudicia tua a facie eius: omnium inimicorum suorum dominabitur.

27 (6). Dixit enim in corde suo: Non movebor a generatione in generationem, sine malo.

28 (7). Cuius maledictione os plenum est, et amaritudine, et dolo: sub lingua eius labor et dolor.

29 (8). Sedet in insidiis cum divitibus in occultis, ut interficiat innocentem.

30 (9). Oculi eius in pauperem respiciunt: insidiatur in abscondito, quasi leo in spelunca sua.

Insidiatur ut rapiat pauperem: rapere pauperem dum adtrahit eum.

31 (10). In laqueo suo humiliabit eum, inclinabit se, et cadet cum dominatus fuerit pauperum.

32 (11). Dixit enim in corde suo: Oblitus est Deus, avertit faciem suam ne videat in finem.

33 (12). Exsurge, Domine Deus, exaltetur manus tua: ne obliviscaris pauperum.

34 (13). Propter quid inritavit impius Deum? Dixit enim in corde suo: Non requiret.

35 (14). Vides, quoniam tu laborem et dolorem consideras: ut tradas eos in manus tuas.

Tibi derelictus est pauper: orfano tu **eris** (W, eras) adiutor.

36 (15). Contere brachium peccatoris et maligni: quaeretur peccatum illius, et non invenietur.

37 (16). Dominus regnabit in aeternum, et in saeculum saeculi: peribitis, gentes, de terra illius.

38 (17). Desiderium pauperum exaudivit Dominus: praeparationem cordis eorum audivit auris tua.

39 (18). Iudicare pupillo et humili, ut non adponat ultra magnificare se homo super terram.

Psalm 10

1. In finem, Psalmus David.

2. In Domino confido: quomodo dicitis animae meae: Transmigra in **montem** (W, montes) sicut passer?

3. Quoniam ecce peccatores intenderunt arcum, paraverunt sagittas suas in faretra, ut sagittent in obscuro rectos corde.

4. Quoniam quae perfecisti, destruxerunt: iustus autem quid fecit?

5. Dominus in templo sancto suo, Dominus in caelo sedis eius.

Oculi eius in pauperem respiciunt: palpebrae eius interrogant filios hominum.

6. Dominus interrogat iustum et impium: qui autem diligit iniquitatem, odit animam suam.

7. Pluet super peccatores laqueos: ignis et sulphur et spiritus procellarum pars calicis eorum.

8. Quoniam iustus Dominus et iustitias dilexit: aequitatem vidit vultus eius.

Psalm 11

1. In finem pro octava, Psalmus David.

2. Salvum me fac, Domine, quoniam defecit sanctus: quoniam deminutae sunt veritates a filiis hominum.

3. Vana locuti sunt unusquisque ad proximum suum: labia dolosa, in corde et corde locuti sunt.

4. Disperdat Dominus universa labia dolosa, **et** (W, omit et) linguam magniloquam.

5. Qui dixerunt: Linguam nostram magnificabimus, labia nostra a nobis sunt, quis noster Dominus est?

6. Propter miseriam inopum, et gemitum pauperum, nunc exsurgam, dicit Dominus.

Ponam in salutari: fiducialiter agam in eo.

7. Eloquia Domini, eloquia casta argentum igne examinatum, probatum terrae, purgatum septuplum.

8. Tu, Domine, servabis nos: et custodies nos a generatione hac in aeternum.

9. In circuitu impii ambulant: secundum altitudinem tuam multiplicasti filios hominum.

Psalm 12

1. In finem, Psalmus David.

Usquequo, Domine, oblivisceris me in finem? Usquequo avertis faciem tuam a me?

2. Quamdiu ponam consilia in anima mea, dolorem in corde meo per diem?

3. Usquequo exaltabitur inimicus meus super me?

4. Respice, **et** (W, omit et) exaudi me, Domine Deus meus.

Inlumina oculos meos ne umquam obdormiam in **morte** (W, mortem):

5. Nequando dicat inimicus meus: Praevalui adversus eum.

Qui tribulant me, exultabunt si motus fuero:

6. Ego autem in misericordia tua speravi.

Exultabit cor meum in salutari tuo: cantabo Domino qui bona tribit mihi: et psallam nomini Domini altissimi.

Psalm 13

1. In finem, Psalmus David.
Dixit insipiens in corde suo: Non est Deus.
Corrupti sunt, et abominabiles facti sunt in studiis suis: non est qui faciat bonum, non est usque ad unum.

2. Dominus de caelo prospexit super filios hominum, ut videat si est intellegens, aut requirens Deum.

3. Omnes declinaverunt, simul inutiles facti sunt: non est qui faciat bonum, non est usque ad unum.
Sepulchrum patens est guttur eorum: linguis suis dolose agebant, venenum aspidum sub labiis eorum.
Quorum os maledictione et amaritudine plenum est: veloces pedes eorum ad effundendum sanguinem.
Contritio et infelicitas in viis eorum, et viam pacis non cognoverunt: non est timor Dei ante oculos eorum.

4. Nonne cognoscent omnes qui operantur iniquitatem, qui devorant plebem meam sicut escam panis?

5. Dominum non invocaverunt, illic trepidaverunt timore, ubi non erat timor.

6. Quoniam **Dominus** (W, Deus) in generatione iusta **est**, (W, omit est) consilium inopis confudistis: quoniam Dominus spes eius est.

7. Quis dabit ex Sion salutare Israhel? Cum averterit Dominus captivitatem plebis suae, exultabit Iacob, et laetabitur Israhel.

Psalm 14

1. Psalmus David
Domine, quis habitabit in tabernaculo tuo? Aut quis requiescet in monte sancto tuo?

2. Qui ingreditur sine macula, et operatur iustitiam:

3. Qui loquitur veritatem in corde suo, qui non egit dolum in lingua sua:

34

Nec fecit proximo suo malum, et obprobrium non accepit adversus proximos suos.

4. Ad nihilum deductus est in conspectu eius malignus: timentes autem Dominum glorificat:

Qui iurat proximo suo, et non decipit,

5. Qui pecuniam suam non dedit ad usuram, et munera super **innocentem** (W, innocentes) non accepit.

Qui facit haec, non movebitur in aeternum.

Psalm 15

1. Tituli inscriptio ipsi David.

Conserva me, Domine, quoniam in te speravi.

2. Dixi Domino: **Deus** (Dominus) meus es tu, quoniam bonorum meorum non eges.

3. Sanctis, qui sunt in terra eius, mirificavit (W, add mihi) omnes voluntates meas in eis.

4. Multiplicatae sunt infirmitates eorum: postea adceleraverunt.

Non congregabo conventicula eorum de sanguinibus: nec memor ero nominum eorum per labia mea.

5. Dominus pars hereditatis meae, et calicis mei: tu es, qui restitues hereditatem meam mihi.

6. Funes ceciderunt mihi in praeclaris: etenim hereditas mea praeclara est mihi.

7. Benedicam Dominum, qui tribuit mihi intellectum: insuper et usque ad noctem **increpuerunt** (W, increpaverunt) me renes mei.

8. Providebam Dominum in conspectu meo semper: quoniam a dextris est mihi, ne commovear.

9. Propter hoc laetatum est cor meum, et exultavit lingua mea: insuper et caro mea requiescet in spe.

10. Quoniam non derelinques animam meam in inferno: **nec** (W, non) dabis sanctum tuum videre corruptionem.

Notas mihi fecisti vias vitae, adimplebis me laetitia cum vultu tuo: **delectationes** (W, delectatio) in dextera tua usque in finem.

Psalm 18

1. In finem, Psalmus David.

2. Caeli enarrant gloriam Dei, et opera manuum eius adnuntiat firmamentum.

3. Dies diei eructat verbum, et nox nocti indicat scientiam.

4. Non sunt loquellae, neque sermones, quorum non audiantur voces eorum.

5. In omnem terram exivit sonus eorum: et in fines orbis terrae verba eorum.

6. In sole posuit tabernaculum suum: et ipse tamquam sponsus procedens de thalamo suo:

exultavit ut gigans ad currendam viam, (W, add suam).

7. a summo coelo egressio eius:

et occursus eius usque ad summum eius: nec est qui se abscondat a calore eius.

8. Lex Domini inmaculata convertens animas: testimonium Domini fidele, sapientiam praestans parvulis.

9. Iustitiae Domini rectae, laetificantes corda: praeceptum Domini lucidum, inluminans oculos.

10. Timor Domini sanctus, permanens in saeculum saeculi: iudicia Domini vera, iustificata in semet ipsa.

11. Desiderabilia super aurum et lapidem pretiosum multum: et dulciora super mel et favum.

12. Etenim servus tuus custodit ea, in custodiendis illis retributio multa.

13. Delicta quis intellegit? Ab occultis meis munda me:

14. Et ab alienis parce servo tuo.

Si mei non fuerint dominati, tunc inmaculatus ero: et emundabor a delicto maximo.

15. Et erunt ut conplaceant eloquia oris mei: et meditatio cordis mei in conspectu tuo semper. Domine adiutor meus, et redemptor meus.

Psalm 19

1. In finem, Psalmus David.

2. Exaudiat te Dominus in die tribulationis: protegat te nomen Dei Iacob.

3. Mittat tibi auxilium de sancto: et de Sion tueatur te.

4. Memor sit omnis sacrificii tui: et holocaustum tuum pingue fiat.

Diapsalma

5. Tribuat tibi secundum cor tuum: et omne consilium tuum confirmet.

6. Laetabimur in salutari tuo: et in nomine Dei nostri magnificabimur.

7. Impleat Dominus omnes petitiones tuas: nunc cognovi quoniam salvum fecit Dominus Christum suum.

Exaudiet illum de caelo sancto suo: in potentatibus salus dexterae eius.

8. Hii in curribus, et hii in equis: nos autem in nomine Domini Dei nostri invocabimus.

9. Ipsi obligati sunt, et ceciderunt: nos **autem** (W, vero) surreximus et erecti sumus.

10. Domine, salvum fac regem: et exaudi nos in die, qua invocaverimus te.

Psalm 22

1. Psalmus David.

Dominus **regit** (W, reget) me, et nihil mihi deerit.

2. In loco pascuae ibi me conlocavit.

Super aquam refectionis educavit me:

3. Animam meam convertit.

Deduxit me super semitas iustitae, propter nomen suum.

4. Nam, et si ambulavero in medio umbrae mortis, non timebo mala: quoniam tu mecum es.

Virga tua, et baculus tuus, ipsa me consolata sunt.

5. Parasti in conspectu meo mensam, adversus eos, qui tribulant me.

Inpinguasti in oleo caput meum: et calix meus inebrians quam praeclarus est:

6. Et misericordia tua subsequitur me omnibus diebus vitae meae.

7. Et ut inhabitem in domo Domini, in longitudinem dierum.

Psalm 23

1. Psalmus David. Prima sabbati.

Domini est terra, et plenitudo eius: orbis terrarum, et universi, qui habitant in eo.

2. Quia ipse super maria fundavit eum: et super flumina praeparavit eum.

3. Quis ascendit in montem Domini? Aut quis stabit in loco sancto eius?

4. Innocens manibus et mundo corde, qui non accepit in vano animam suam, nec iuravit in dolo proximo suo.

5. Hic accipiet benedictionem a Domino: et misericordiam a Deo **salutari** (W, salvatore) suo.

6. Haec est generatio quaerentium eum, quaerentium faciem Dei Iacob.

Diapsalma

7. Adtollite portas, principes, vestras, et elevamini, portae aeternales: et introibit rex gloriae.

8. Quis est iste rex gloriae? Dominus fortis, et potens: Dominus potens in proelio.

9. Adtollite portas, principes, vestras, et elevamini, portae aeternales: et introibit rex gloriae.

10. Quis est iste rex gloriae? Dominus virtutum ipse est rex gloriae.

Psalm 25

1. Psalmus David.

Iudica me, Domine, quoniam ego in innocentia mea ingressus sum: et in Domino sperans non infirmabor.

2. Proba me, Domine, et tempta me: ure renes meos et cor meum.

3. Quoniam misericorida tua ante oculos meos est: et conplacui in veritate tua.

4. Non sedi cum concilio vanitatis: et cum iniqua gerentibus non introibo.

5. Odivi ecclesiam malignantium: et cum impiis non sedebo.

6. Lavabo inter innocentes manus meas: et circumdabo altare tuum, Domine:

7. Ut audiam vocem laudis, et enarrem universa mirabilia tua.

8. Domine, dilexi decorem domus tuae, et locum habitationis gloriae tuae.

9. Ne perdas cum impiis, **Deus** (W, omit Deus), animam meam, et cum viris sanguinum vitam meam:

10. In quorum manibus iniquitates sunt: dextera eorum repleta est muneribus.

11. Ego autem in innocentia mea ingressus sum: redime me, et miserere mei.

12. Pes meus stetit in directo: in ecclesiis benedicam te, Domine.

Psalm 31

1. **Ipsi** (W, Huic) David intellectus.

Beati, quorum remissae sunt iniquitates: et quorum tecta sunt peccata.

2. Beatus vir, cui non **inputavit** (W, inputabit) Dominus peccatum, nec est in spiritu eius dolus.

3. Quoniam tacui, inveteraverunt ossa mea, dum clamarem tota die.

4. Quoniam die ac nocte gravata est super me manus tua: conversus sum in aerumna mea, dum configitur (W, add mihi) spina.
Diapsalma

5. Delictum meum cognitum tibi feci: et iniustitiam meam non abscondi.

Dixi: confitebor adversum me iniustitiam meam Domino: et tu remisisti impietatem peccati mei.
Diapsalma

6. Pro hac orabit ad te omnis sanctus, in tempore oportuno.

Verumtamen in diluvio aquarum multarum, ad eum non adproximabunt.

7. Tu es refugium meum a tribulatione, quae cirumdedit me: exultatio mea, erue me a circumdantibus me.
Diapsalma

8. Intellectum tibi dabo, et instruam te in via hac, qua gradieris: firmabo super te oculos meos.

9. Nolite fieri sicut equus et mulus, quibus non est intellectus.

In camo et freno maxillas eorum constringe, qui non approximant ad te.

10. Multa flagella peccatoris, sperantem autem in Domino misericordia circumdabit.

11. Laetamini in Domino et exultate, iusti, et gloriamini, omnes recti corde.

Psalm 37

1. Psalmus David, in rememorationem de sabbato.

2. Domine, ne in furore tuo arguas me, neque in ira tua corripias me.

3. Quoniam sagittae tuae infixae sunt mihi: et confirmasti super me manum tuam.

4. Non est sanitas **in carne mea** (W, carni meae) a facie irae tuae: non est pax ossibus meis a facie peccatorum meorum.

5. Quoniam iniquitates meae supergressae sunt caput meum: sicut onus grave gravatae sunt super me.

6. Putruerunt et corruptae sunt cicatrices meae, a facie insipientiae meae.

7. Miser factus sum et curvatus sum usque **in** (W, ad) finem: tota die contristatus ingrediebar.

8. Quoniam lumbi mei impleti sunt inlusionibus: et non est sanitas in carne mea.

9. Adflictus sum, et humiliatus sum nimis: rugiebam a gemitu cordis mei.

10. Domine, ante te omne desiderium meum: et gemitus meus a te non est absconditus.

11. Cor meum conturbatum est, dereliquit me virtus mea: et lumen oculorum meorum, et ipsum non est mecum.

12. Amici mei et proximi mei adversus me adpropinquaverunt, et steterunt. Et qui iuxta me erant, de longe steterunt.

13. et vim faciebant qui quaerebant animam meam.

Et qui inquirebant mala mihi, locuti sunt vanitates: et dolos tota die meditabantur.

14. Ego autem tamquam surdus non audiebam: et sicut mutus non aperiens os suum.

15. Et factus sum sicut homo non audiens: et non habens in ore suo redargutiones.

16. Quoniam in te, Domine, speravi: tu exaudies **me** (W, omit me), Domine Deus meus.

17. Quia dixi: Nequando supergaudeant mihi inimici mei: et dum commoventur pedes mei, super me magna locuti sunt.

18. Quoniam ego in flagella paratus **sum** (W, omit sum): et dolor meus in conspectu meo semper.

19. Quoniam iniquitatem meam adnuntiabo: et cogitabo pro peccato meo.

20. Inimici autem mei **vivunt** (W, vivent), et **confirmati** (W, firmati) sunt super me: et multiplicati sunt qui oderunt me inique.

21. Qui retribuunt mala pro bonis, detrahebant mihi: quoniam sequebar bonitatem.

22. **Ne** (W, non) derelinquas me, Domine Deus meus: ne discesseris a me.

23. Intende in adiutorium meum, Domine **Deus** (W, omit Deus) salutis meae.

Psalm 38

1. In finem, ipsi Idithun, Canticum David.

2. Dixi: Custodiam vias meas: ut non delinquam in lingua mea.
Posui ori meo custodiam, cum consisteret peccator adversum me.

3. Obmutui, et humiliatus sum, et silui a bonis: et dolor meus renovatus est.

4. Concaluit cor meum intra me: et in meditatione mea exardescet ignis.

5. Locutus sum in lingua mea: Notum fac mihi, Domine, finem meum,
et numerum dierum meorum quis est: ut sciam quid desit mihi.

6. Ecce mensurabiles posuisti dies meos: et substantia mea tamquam nihilum ante te.
Verumtamen universa vanitas, omnis homo vivens.
Diapsalma

7. Verumtamen in imagine pertransit homo: sed et frustra conturbatur.
Thesaurizat: et ignorat cui congregabit ea.

8. Et nunc quae est expectatio mea? Nonne Dominus? Et substantia mea apud te est.

9. Ab omnibus iniquitatibus meis erue me: obprobrium insipienti dedisti me.

10. Obmutui, et non aperui os meum, quoniam tu fecisti:

11. amove a me plagas tuas.

12. A fortitudine manus tuae ego defeci in increpationibus: propter iniquitatem corripuisti hominem.

Et tabescere fecisti sicut araneam animam eius: verumtamen vane conturbatur omnis homo.

Diapsalma

13. Exaudi orationem meam, Domine, et deprecationem meam: auribus percipe lacrimas meas.

Ne sileas: quoniam advena ego sum apud te, et peregrinus, sicut omnes patres mei.

14. Remitte mihi, ut refrigerer priusquam abeam, et amplius non ero.

Psalm 41

1. In finem, **Intellectus** (W, In intellectum) filiis Core.

2. Quemadmodum desiderat cervus ad fontes aquarum: ita desiderat anima mea ad te, Deus.

3. Sitivit anima mea ad Deum fortem vivum: quando veniam et **adparebo** (W, parebo) ante faciem Dei?

4. Fuerunt mihi lacrimae meae **panes** (W, panis) die ac nocte: dum dicitur mihi cotidie: Ubi est Deus tuus?

5. Haec recordatus sum, et effudi in me animam meam: Quoniam transibo in **locum** (W, loco) tabernaculi admirabilis, usque ad domum Dei:

In voce exultationis et confessionis: sonus epulantis.

6. Quare tristis es, anima mea? Et quare conturbas me?

Spera in Deo, quoniam **adhuc** (W, omit adhuc) confitebor illi: salutare vultus mei,

7. **et** (W, omit et) Deus meus.

Ad me ipsum anima mea conturbata est: propterea memor ero tui de terra Iordanis, et Hermoniim a monte modico.

8. Abyssus ad abyssum invocat, in voce cataractarum tuarum.

Omnia excelsa tua, et fluctus tui super me transierunt.

9. In die mandavit Dominus misericordiam suam: et nocte canticum eius.

Apud me oratio Deo vitae meae.

10. dicam Deo: Susceptor meus es,

quare oblitus es mei? **Et** (W, omit et) quare contristatus incedo, dum adfligit me inimicus?

11. Dum confringuntur ossa mea, exprobraverunt mihi qui tribulant me **inimici mei** (W, omit inimici mei)

Dum dicunt mihi per singulos dies: Ubi est Deus tuus?

12. Quare tristis es, anima mea? et quare conturbas me?

Spera in **Deo** (W, Deum), quoniam adhuc confitebor illi: salutare vultus mei, et Deus meus.

Psalm 42

1. Psalmus David.

Iudica me, Deus, et discerne causam meam de gente non sancta, ab homine iniquo et doloso erue me.

2. Quia tu es, Deus, fortitudo mea: quare me reppulisti? Quare tristis incedo, dum adfligit me inimicus?

3. Emitte lucem tuam et veritatem tuam: ipsa me deduxerunt, et adduxerunt in montem sanctum tuum, et in tabernacula tua.

4. Et intoibo ad altare Dei: ad Deum, qui laetificat iuventutem meam.

Confitebor tibi in cithara, Deus Deus meus:

5. Quare tristis es, anima mea? et quare conturbas me

Spera in **Deo** (W, Deum), quoniam adhuc confitebor illi: salutare vultus mei, et Deus meus.

Psalm 50

1. In finem, Psalmus David.

2. cum venit ad eum Nathan Propheta, quando intravit ad Bethsabee.

3. Miserere mei, Deus, secundum magnam misericordiam tuam.

Et secundum multitudinem miserationum tuarum, dele iniquitatem meam.

4. Amplius lava me ab iniquitate mea: et a peccato meo munda me.

5. Quoniam iniquitatem meam ego cognosco: et peccatum meum contra me est semper.

6. Tibi soli peccavi, et malum coram te feci: ut iustificeris in sermonibus tuis, et vincas cum iudicaris.

7. Ecce enim in iniquitatibus conceptus sum: et in peccatis concepit me mater mea.

8. Ecce enim veritatem dilexisti: incerta et occulta sapientiae tuae manifestasti mihi.

9. Asparges me hysopo, et mundabor: lavabis me, et super nivem dealbabor.

10. Auditui meo dabis gaudium et laetitam: **et** (W, omit et) exultabunt ossa humiliata.

11. Averte faciem tuam a peccatis meis: et omnes iniquitates meas dele.

12. Cor mundum crea in me, Deus: et spiritum rectum innova in visceribus meis.

13. Ne proicias me a facie tua: et spiritum sanctum tuum ne auferas a me.

14. Redde mihi laetitiam salutaris tui: et spiritu principali confirma me.

15. Docebo iniquos vias tuas: et impii ad te convertentur.

16. Libera me de sanguinibus, Deus, Deus salutis meae: **et** (W, omit et) exultabit lingua mea iustitiam tuam.

17. Domina, labia mea aperies: et os meum adnuntiabit laudem tuam.

18. Quoniam si voluisses sacrificium dedissem utique: holocaustis non delectaberis.

19. Sacrificium Deo spiritus contribulatus: cor contritum, et humiliatum, Deus, non **despicies** (W, spernet).

20. Benigne fac, Domine, in bona voluntate tua Sion: **ut** (W, et) aedificentur muri Hierusalem.

21. Tunc acceptabis sacrificium iustitiae, oblations, et holocausta: tunc inponent super altare tuum vitulos.

Psalm 109

1. Psalmus David.
Dixit Dominus Domino meo: Sede a dextris meis:
Donec ponam inimicos tuos, scabillum pedum tuorum.

2. Virgam virtutis tuae emittet Dominus ex Sion: dominare in medio inimicorum tuorum.

3. Tecum principium in die virtutis tuae in splendoribus sanctorum: ex utero ante luciferum genui te.

4. Iuravit Dominus et non paenitebit eum: Tu es sacerdos in aeternum secundum ordinem Melchisedech.

5. Dominus a dextris tuis, confregit in die irae suae reges.

6. Iudicabit in nationibus, implebit **ruinas** (W, cadavera): conquassabit capita in terra multorum.

7. De torrente in via bibet: propterea exaltabit caput.

Psalm 119

1. Canticum graduum.
Ad Dominum cum tribularer clamavi: et exaudivit me.

2. Domine, libera animam meam a labiis iniquis, a lingua dolosa.

3. Quid detur tibi, **aut** (W, et) quid adponatur tibi ad linguam dolosam?

4. Sagittae potentis acutae, cum carbonibus desolatoriis.

5. Heu mihi, quia incolatus meus prolongatus est: habitavi cum **habitantibus** (habitantionibus) Cedar:

6. multum incola fuit anima mea.

7. Cum his qui oderant pacem, eram pacificus: cum loquebar illis, inpugnabant me gratis.

Psalm 121

1. Canticum graduum (W, add huic David).
Laetatus sum in his, quae dicta sunt mihi: In domum Domini ibimus.

2. Stantes erant pedes nostri, in atriis tuis, Hierusalem.

3. Hierusalem, quae aedificatur ut civitas: cuius participatio eius in id ipsum.

4. Illic enim ascenderunt tribus, tribus Domini: testimonium Israhel ad confitendum nomini Domini.

5. Quia illic sederunt sedes in iudicium, sedes super domum David.

6. Rogate quae ad pacem sunt Hierusalem: et abundantia diligentibus te.

7. Fiat pax in virtute tua: et abundantia in turribus tuis.

8. Propter fratres meos, et proximos meos, loquebar pacem de te:

9. Propter domum Domini Dei nostri, quaesivi bona tibi.

Psalm 122

Canticum graduum

1. Ad te levavi oculos meos, qui habitas in **caelis** (W, caelo).

2. Ecce sicut oculi servorum, in manibus dominorum suorum, sicut oculi ancillae in manibus dominae **suae** (W, eius): ita oculi nostri ad Dominum Deum nostrum, donec misereatur nostri.

3. Miserere nostri, Domine, miserere nostri: quia multum repleti sumus despectione.

4. Quia multum repleta est anima nostra: obprobrium abundantibus, et despectio superbis.

Psalm 123

1. Canticum graduum (W, add huic David).

Nisi quia Dominus erat in nobis, dicat nunc Israhel:

2. nisi quia Dominus erat in nobis, cum exsurgerent in nos homines,

3. forte vivos deglutissent nos: cum irasceretur furor eorum in nos,

4. forsitan aqua absorbuisset nos.

5. Torrentem pertransivit anima nostra: forsitan pertransisset anima nostra aquam intolerabilem.

6. Benedictus Dominus, qui non dedit nos in captionem dentibus eorum.

7. Anima nostra sicut passer erepta est de laqueo venantium: laqueus contritus est, et nos liberati sumus.

8. Adiutorium nostrum in nomine Domini, qui fecit caelum et terram.

Psalm 125

1. Canticum graduum

In convertendo **Dominus** (W, Dominum) captivitatem Sion: facti sumus sicut consolati:

2. Tunc repletum est gaudio os nostrum: et lingua nostra exultatione. Tunc dicent inter gentes: Magnificavit Dominus facere cum eis.

3. Magnificavit Dominus facere nobiscum: facti sumus laetantes.

4. Converte, Domine, captivitatem nostram, sicut torrens in austro.

5. Qui seminant in lacrimis, in exultatione metent.

6. Euntes ibant et flebant, **mittentes** (W, portantes) semina sua.

Venientes autem venient cum exultatione, portantes manipiulos suos.

Psalm 126

1. Canticum graduum Salomonis. Nisi Dominus aedificaverit domum, in vanum laboraverunt qui aedificant eam.

Nisi Dominus custodierit civitatem, frustra vigilat qui custodit **eam** (W, omit eam).

2. Vanum est vobis ante lucem surgere: **surgite** (W, surgere) postquam sederitis, qui manducatis panem doloris. Cum dederit dilectis suis somnum:

3. ecce hereditas Domini, filii, mercis, fructus ventris.

4. Sicut sagittae in manu potentis: ita filii excussorum.

5. Beatus vir qui implebit desiderium suum ex ipsis: non confundentur cum loquentur inimicis suis in porta.

Psalm 127

1. Canticum graduum.

Beati omnes, qui timent Dominum, qui ambulant in viis eius.

2. Labores manuum tuarum quia manducabis: beatus es, et bene tibi erit.

3. Uxor tua sicut vitis abundans, in lateribus domus tuae.

Filii tui sicut novellae olivarum, in circuitu mensae tuae.

4. Ecce sic benedicetur homo, qui timet Dominum.

5. Benedicat **tibi** (W, te) Dominus ex Sion: et videas bona Hierusalem omnibus diebus vitae tuae.

6. Et videas filios filiorum tuorum, **pacem** (W, pax) super Israhel.

Psalm 128

1. Canticum graduum.

Saepe expugnaverunt me a iuventute mea: dicat nunc Israhel.

2. Saepe expugnaverunt me a iuventute mea: etenim non potuerunt mihi.

3. Supra dorsum meum **fabricaverunt** (W, fabricabantur) peccatores: prolongaverunt iniquitatem suam.

4. Dominus iustus concidet cervices peccatorum:

5. Confundantur et convertantur retrorsum omnes, qui oderunt Sion.

6. Fiant sicut faenum tectorum: quod priusquam evellatur, exaruit:

7. De quo non implevit manum suam qui metit, et sinum suum qui manipulos colligit:

8. et non dixerunt qui praeteribant: Benedictio Domini super vos: benediximus vobis in nomine Domini.

Psalm 129

1. Canticum graduum.

De profundis clamavi ad te, Domine:

2. Domine, exaudi vocem meam. Fiant aures tuae intendentes, in vocem deprecationis meae.

3. Si iniquitates observabis, Domine: Domine, quis sustinebit?

4. Quia apud te propitiatio est: **et** (W, omit et) propter legem tuam sustinui te, Domine.

Sustinuit anima mea in **verbo** (W, verbum) eius:

5. speravit anima mea in Domino.

6. A custodia matutina usque ad noctem speret Israhel in Domino

7. Quia apud Dominum misericordia: et copiosa apud eum redemptio

8. Et ipse redimet Israhel, ex omnibus iniquitatibus eius.

Psalm 130

1. Canticum graduum David.

Domine, non est exaltatum cor meum neque elati sunt oculi mei.

Neque ambulavi in magnis, neque in mirabilibus super me.

2. Si non humiliter sentiebam: sed exaltavi animam meam:

sicut **ablactatus est** (W, ablactatum) super matrem suam, ita retributio in anima mea.

3. Speret Israhel in Domino, ex hoc nunc et usque in saeculum.

Psalm 132

1. Canticum graduum David.

Ecce quam bonum, et quam iucundum habitare fratres in unum:

2. Sicut unguentum in capite, quod descendit in barbam, barbam Aaron, quod descendit in ora vestimenti eius:

3. Sicut ros Hermon, qui descendit in **montem** (W, montes) Sion.

Quoniam illic mandavit Dominus benedictionem, et vitam usque in saeculum.

Psalm 150

1. Alleluia.

Laudate Dominum in sanctis eius: laudate eum in firmamento virtutis eius.

2. Laudate eum in virtutibus eius: laudate eum secundum multitudinem magnitudinis eius.

3. Laudate eum in sono tubae: laudate eum in psalterio et cithara.

4. Laudate eum in tympano et choro: laudate eum in cordis et organo.

5. Laudate eum in cymbalis bene sonantibus: laudate eum in cymbalis iubilationis:

omnis spiritus laudet Dominum.

Commentary

Psalm 1

In Christian tradition, Psalm 1 was viewed as both compendium and prologue to the whole collection. To Chrysologus, bishop of Ravenna, it was the Psalm of Psalms, the key to the mystery of all the Psalms; to Jerome, it was the preface of the Holy Spirit.

1.1　　**Beatus vir qui:** The formula occurs in literature that has wisdom as its theme (e.g. *Proverbs*) and thus sets the didactic tone of the Psalm.

Beatus: May refer, as in classical Latin, to a human or divine being; corresponds here to the Hebrew secular congratulatory 'ašrê, 'happy' (literally, 'O the happiness of'), which is never used of God. Elsewhere *beatus* may translate the cultic-sacral bārûk.

vir: Latin would idiomatically omit the substantive. *Vir* = 'anyone' reflects the Greek of LXX which reproduces Hebrew idiom. Some exegetes explained its presence by a special paradigmatic significance: 'the (ideal) Man', i.e. Christ; hence the Psalm's Christological interpretation. In fact, the definite article with 'îš may make it exactly = *vir*, 'the ideal mature male'. In Hebrew poetry the precise use of the article is often elusive.

abiit: Either 'go away, depart' (from the right path) or simply 'go about, walk' in an ethical sense: 'live, conduct oneself', a Hebraism. Cf. 25.1 *ego in innocentia mea ingressus sum*. 'I have led a blameless life.' The use of the compound verb (*abire*) for the simple (*ire*) is common in V. In general, in Vulgar Latin the prefixed preposition often merely reinforces the sense of the simple verb. The perfects *abiit, stetit, sedit* reproduce three Greek aorists which, in this gnomic context, might have been translated as presents. The underlying Hebrew perfects are characterizing and describe actions resulting in states. In classical Latin, gnomic perfects are rare.

in consilio: Either modal, 'according to the counsel' or motion towards, 'into the council'. In later Latin the distinction between directional '*in*' with the accusative and static '*in*' with the ablative is blurred.

51

peccatorum: A post-classical word whose origin is sometimes attributed (probably too precisely) to Tertullian.

cathedra pestilentiae: The Latin suggests the image of a teacher in his chair who imparts harmful doctrine to his students. Abstract *pestilentiae* is used for concrete *pestiferorum* as is LXX's λοιμῶν ('of pests'). Cf. English 'pest' or 'plague' to refer to a person. The Hebrew word for 'chair' may also mean 'session, assembly', and the MT here may be rendered 'assembly of mockers (of God)'. Cf. Jer. *cathedra derisorum.*

abiit, stetit, sedit: Traditionally regarded as three progressive stages of evil, 'walk, stand, sit', but also to the Oriental mind emphasizing the total dimensionality of sin. Note the parallelism of thought and phraseology which is a major characteristic of Hebrew poetry.

1.2   **lege:** Hebrew tôrāh which may refer not only to the Mosaic 'law' but more generally in some contexts to the revelation of God's will. In Christian Latin, *lex* may refer to God's law, written or unwritten, or even to Christianity itself.

Domini: *Dominus*, 'the Lord', translates LXX's κύριος which in turn may ultimately reflect a Palestinian custom of pronouncing the sacred Tetragrammation YHWH, ʾādôn 'lord'. In Christian Latin, it may refer equally to God the Father or Jesus the Son.

voluntas: Not 'desire', but, by metonymy 'object of desire, predilection, pleasure'. Following ultimately Hebrew idiom, the verb 'to be' is omitted.

meditabitur: Either 'meditate' or 'exercise oneself, actively practice'. Cf. the use of *meditationes* for Roman military exercises. From the Hebrew perspective, study and practice merge into one. The Hebrew verb (hāgāh) means 'to murmur over', i.e. read privately but not silently. Even in Christianity, *meditatio* involved not only interior reflection on a text, but its active repetition aloud. The future tense renders the Greek future which crudely reproduces the Hebrew imperfect. The present tense would more accurately have rendered the original since here it is characterizing. The Hebrew imperfect represents action or state not completed whether in past, present or (very commonly) future time.

die ac nocte Should mean 'in a day and a night', but here the Latin is following the Greek's too literal translation of the Hebrew; properly = *diem noctemque* or *dies noctesque*, 'day and night, constantly'.

1.3   **Et** The Hebrew conjunction = 'and' is often rendered literally though it has in fact various uses. Here, for example, it may be emphatic or consequential: 'So then ... .'

lignum In classical prose 'wood' or 'stump'; then by metonymy 'tree'; often used also of Christ's 'cross' or for Christ Himself as 'the tree of life'.

plantatum The Hebrew more exactly = *transplantatum*.

secus Usually an adverb in classical Latin but in later Latin a preposition, 'by, beside' = Greek παρά.

decursus Artificial 'channels'.

aquarum The plural probably reflects Hebrew idiom, but *aqua* = *aquae* is a colloquialism of later Latin. The 'waters' in Christian exegesis are sometimes interpreted as baptismal.

faciet For classical future perfect.

prosperabuntur 'will succeed'. The verb, with few exceptions, is deponent in V.

1.4   **Non sic impii non sic** sc. *sunt*. The emphatic repetition occurs in LXX not MT. So also, *a facie terrae* below.

pulvis 'dust', but in MT 'chaff', the image being derived from winnowing in which the wheat is separated from the chaff by the action of the winds.

1.5   **Ideo** Either prospective, 'for this reason (namely)' *quoniam novit*; or, as Augustine interprets, retrospective, 'because, like dust, they are cast off from the face of the earth, therefore ... .'

resurgent ... in iudicio Hebrew 'will stand in judgement', i.e. 'will win their cases', a sense possible in both the Hebrew and Latin, but Augustine's remark that *in consilio iustorum* is parallel to *in iudicio* probably exactly recovers the original Hebrew sense. The meaning 'stand' has sometimes been forced on *resurgere* by the rule of compound verb for simple. More probably the translator had in mind resurrection and not every act of judgement by which God separates the righteous from the evil, but rather the Last Judgement. Cf. also LXX, ἀναστήσονται. Augustine poses an alternative sense: the *impii*, differing from general *peccatores,* 'will indeed rise, but not to be judged, since they have already been appointed to very fixed penalties'.

1.6   **novit** 'recognizes', hence 'approves'. The Hebrew verb expresses not merely intellectual knowledge but loving concern and close contact. Semantically broadened, *noscere* exemplifies an *idioma scripturae*. Misunderstanding of it often posed a dilemma for the Church fathers and their concept of an omniscient God, especially in those scriptural contexts where God is said not to know someone or something (e.g. sinners or evil). Cf. also in classical Latin the use of *noscere* to refer to carnal knowledge.

viam ... iter In MT, identical words, referring to 'way' of life, i.e. mode of conduct.

Psalm 2

A royal Psalm which may originally have played some part in the Hebrew king's coronation ceremony, but clear evidence is lacking. In the Acts of the Apostles, Christians regarded it as Messianic with references to Christ and His persecutors, Herod, Pilate, the Gentiles and Israel. In the synoptic gospels, it is connected with Christ's baptism and transfiguration; in Revelation, with Christ's apocalyptic judgement.

2.1   **Psalmus David** This superscription and several slight variants occur 85 times in V, 73 in MT. *David*, treated generally as an indeclinable, may be genitive but possibly also dative. Cf. Ps. 27.1, *Psalmus ipsi David* after LXX's τῷ Δαυείδ which in turn reflects Hebrew l^e dāwîd (literally, 'to David'). l^e, used when the preceding noun is indefinite ('a Psalm'), may denote authorship (by), interest (on behalf of) or relation (concerning). 'David' may also be used generically = a Davidic King, and the superscription may simply classify these Psalms as originally deriving from the royal archives at Jerusalem. Traditional Jewish and Christian interpretation makes the phrase refer to authorship.

fremuerunt *fremo*, 'murmur with discontent'.

gentes 'the nations'. Used in Cicero and Sallust to signify 'strangers, barbarians' in contrast to the *populus Romanus*. Transferred to the religious sphere, it came to be used of 'heathens'. It translates the Greek ἔθνη which similarly was used in Attic inscriptions to refer to foreigners. The Hebrew is gôyîm, and in contemporary Yiddish **goy** = non-Jew. Cf. English 'gentile' which may be used to refer to non-Jews or non-Christians.

populi 'heathen nations', virtually synonymous with *gentes*. The Hebrew, however, might possibly be translated 'warlike peoples', hence 'warriors'. Some Christian exegetes interpreted *populi* = *tribus*, a reference to the 'tribes' of Israel.

meditati sunt Possibly 'have devised, have contemplated'. The underlying Hebrew verb (hāgāh, as in 1.2), however, probably more exactly = 'murmur' since here it is properly parallel to the verb form translated by *fremuerunt*. For this meaning of *meditari*, cf. Isaiah 38.14: *sicut pullus hirundinis si clamabo, meditabor ut columba.*

2.2   **Adstiterunt** 'have stood up (to challenge)'.

terrae in contrast to the king of Israel whose authority derives from God.

principes 'rulers', the usual meaning in post-Augustan prose. Corresponds exactly to the Hebrew word which = 'leader, dignitary'.

in unum 'into a single group, in concert'.

Christum 'the anointed one, the Messiah'. referring originally to the Hebrew king, but in Christian interpretation 'Christ'.

Diapsalma Transliterates the Greek διάψαλμα = Hebrew selāh which does not occur here in MT. An ancient technical term whose meaning is uncertain. Perhaps originally used to mark an interlude of singing or playing some other piece, or to mark the parts where the worshipping congregation were to prostrate themselves.

2.3   **Disrumpamus vincula eorum** Hortatory words spoken by the heathen nations; hence *eorum* refers to the Israelites.

ipsorum = *eorum*. The intensive in later Latin often serves as a weak demonstrative and sometimes is even used for a pure definite article. From it develops the definite article in Sardinian, Provençal and Catalan.

2.4   **caelis** 'heaven', usually singular in classical prose, but here plural after the Greek and Hebrew.

subsannabit 'will mock', a post-classical word.

2.5   **loquetur** The subject is *Dominus*.

ad eos Probably 'against them' rather than 'to them'.

in ira sua Both *in* and the more classical *cum* are used to express manner. The *in* construction reflects the Hebrew.

2.6   **Ego autem** ... In contrast to a problematical Hebrew text, but following the Greek, V makes the king the speaker and not God; *loquetur* then stands unconnected to *ego autem*. *ego autem* corresponds to the Hebrew formula = 'and I' which introduces a resolute self-assertion.

constitutus sum Active in MT, which makes God the speaker, but passive in LXX.

Sion 'Zion'. Note how Hebrew proper names are often treated as indeclinables. In English, Hebrew tsade (ts) is represented by 'z' but in Latin by 's'. Zion originally refers to the hill on which the Solomonic temple was built. Later it designates Jerusalem and its inhabitants and sometimes Israel itself. To Augustine, it stands here for the Church.

praedicans praeceptum eius i.e. proclaiming God's appointment of the speaker as king and the establishment of the Davidic kingdom. To Augustine, the allusion is to preaching, a common meaning of *praedicare* in Christian Latin.

2.7 **Filius meus es tu** Originally a formula of adoption which sealed God's covenant with His earthly king. A divine kingship was not implied.

ego hodie genui te The words are cited by Paul, in Acts of the Apostles, as alluding to the resurrection; by Augustine, as alluding to the eternal, timeless generation of Christ.

2.9 **Reges ... confringes** *reges* 'you will rule' follows the Greek mistranslation of the Hebrew verb meaning 'you will smash'. The Latin thus loses the parallelism between the two Hebrew verbs, both of which essentially = 'break, destroy'.

in virga ferrea For classical ablative of means.

2.10 **Et nunc** Corresponds to a Hebrew adhortatory formula found in Wisdom literature. = 'now then'. On *et*, see on 1.3 *et*.

intellegite 'exercise your understanding, be wise'.

iudicatis 'judge', i.e. 'rule'.

2.11 **in timore** = *cum timore*, expresses manner.

exultate ei Perhaps 'sing praise to Him'. The Hebrew text here is obscure.

2.12 **Adprehendite disciplinam** 'Accept instruction' or 'learn (post-classical meaning) discipline'. The exact meaning of the Hebrew text, with its possible Aramaic elements, remains a crux. Cf. Jer. *adorate pure* and the NIV 'Kiss the Son', both of which derive from a Hebrew root = 'kiss, reverence, worship'.

2.13 **Cum ... eius** The Hebrew clause is usually construed with what precedes: 'For His anger can flare up unexpectedly'. Eschatological preconceptions most likely influenced the translator who had in mind a specific day of wrath and judgement soon to come. 'When in a short while (*in brevi*) His anger will have flashed forth, blessed be all who ... .'

in eo The normal construction with *confidere* in V instead of the classical dative, perhaps because the Hebrew and Greek have prepositions.

Psalm 3

Originally a Psalm of individual lament, in which the speaker prays to God for help and expresses confidence in His deliverance.

3.1   **cum fugeret a facie Abessalon filii sui** An historical note or superscription perhaps interpolated into the Hebrew text to provide the Psalm with a context from David's life. To Augustine, Christ is speaking here and the allusions throughout are to His passion and resurrection. In Roman Catholic ritual this Psalm came to be used in the rite of exorcism.

    a facie = *ab*. In imitation of Hebrew, a preposition and a part of the body is used instead of the simple preposition. Cf. Mark 1.2 *ecce ego mitto angelum meum ante faciem tuam.*

    Abessalon i.e. Absalom, David's rebellious son. V for the most part follows LXX's vocalization of proper names which differs at times from the later Massoretic oral tradition. Augustine interprets the name as *patris pax* and proceeds to comment on the apparent irony.

3.2   **quid** = LXX τί = MT māh. The force of the Hebrew word for 'what' is exclamatory ('how!') but the Latin *quid* in this context is most naturally interpreted as interrogative ('why?'). *Quam* would have been a better translation.

3.3   **animae meae** = *mihi*. The Hebrew word translated 'soul' (nepeš) is sometimes used with a personal suffix in place of a personal pronoun. The dative here is misleading. It reproduces the Greek dative which in turn represents the Hebrew l$^\theta$ + soul + personal suffix. But l$^\theta$ here is not simply 'to', but rather 'in reference to'. *De me* then would have been an idiomatic rendering.

    ipsi = *ei*. The intensive functions here as a weak demonstrative. The shift to the third person appears awkward only because of the dative mistranslation, *animae meae.*

3.4   **Tu autem** Emphatic and in opposition to *multi dicunt. Autem* accurately translates the Hebrew word literally = 'and'.

susceptor In Christian Latin, 'protector, defender', but earlier, 'tax collector' or even 'one who receives or harbours thieves'. In its literal sense 'taker', the word to a Christian would also suggest one of the fundamental mysteries of Christ, *susceptio carnis*, i.e. the Incarnation or Word made flesh; so Augustine, *'quia hominis susceptio est verbum caro factum'*. Hebrew has 'a shield around me'. Out of respect, the LXX and so V tend to alter vivid Hebrew anthropomorphic references to God and comparisons of Him to inanimate objects.

exaltans caput meum = *qui exaltat caput meum*, i.e. the one who supports and raises me up to honor or confidence. The substantival use of the participle ultimately reflects Hebrew idiom. In classical Latin prose, the present participle used as a noun is rare in the nominative case.

3.5 **de monte sancto suo** i.e. from Zion where the ark of the covenant was located. Note *de* in an adverbial local sense.

3.6 **Ego dormivi ... exsurrexi** Taking sleep under such trying circumstances reflects the psalmist's confidence in God. Augustine finds in these words a reference to Christ's passion and resurrection. *Ego* then emphasizes that he did so of His own will.

3.7 **salvum me fac** = *salva me.* The periphrasis with *fac* represents the Hebrew hiphil, an active causative verbal pattern. Thus, in Hebrew the verb 'to be holy' in the hiphil means 'to cause to be holy, to sanctify'.

3.8 **sine causa** Literally, 'without cause, (good) reason' i.e. 'unjustifiably'. The LXX translators have ματαίως, 'without grounds' and so apparently read lᵉ ḥinnam, 'gratuitously'. In MT the text is vocalized leḥî from lᵉḥî, 'jaw, cheek' which is probably correct since it creates a parallel with *dentes*: 'You strike all my enemies on the jaw. You break the teeth of the wicked.'

3.9 **Domini** The word's position is emphatic: salvation is of (from) the Lord, i.e. it is the Lord who gives salvation.

et Supply *sit* or simply repeat *est.*

benedictio 'blessing'. In pagan literature *bene dicere* = εὐφημεῖν, 'use words of good omen, keep a religious silence (in a ritual context)'. *benedicere* = εὐλογεῖν, 'bless' appears in the second century AD in Jewish-Christian contexts.

Psalm 4

Like Ps. 3, originally an individual lament.

4.1 **In finem** Literally, 'unto the end' which some Church fathers interpreted eschatologically or as a reference to Christ after Romans 10.4. *Finis enim legis Christus.* In fact, V here is simply following the LXX rendering which itself is probably a mistranslation of the Hebrew. MT suggests that the obscure technical term found in 55 Psalms may have meant 'for the one who is pre-eminent'. Hence, the traditional but by no means certain translation 'for the chief musician'. The phrase served in some unknown way to classify these Psalms.

   in carminibus Literally, 'in verses'. Again ultimately renders an obscure Hebrew term whose meaning was probably lost in non-Palestinian circles as early as the second century BC. MT seems to allude to the musical instruments with which the Psalm is to be accompanied and is usually translated 'on stringed instruments'.

4.2 **Deus iustitiae meae** Literally, 'the god of my justice' which may mean either 'the God who vindicates my just cause' or simply 'my just God'. Hebrew has few adjectives and so often uses two interdependent nouns where idiomatic Latin would use a noun and adjective; e.g. *vir pacis*, 'peaceful man', *vox orationis meae*, literally, 'sound of my prayer', but properly 'my suppliant voice'. This construction is called a construct chain. Note also the pronominal suffix is attached to the genitive but usually modifies the whole chain. Augustine takes it only with *iustitia*.

   tribulatione 'affliction, tribulation', a post-classical word.

   dilatasti mihi 'You have made room for me', i.e. relieved me. Cf. English 'give someone a breathing space' and Ps. 118.45 *et ambulabam in latitudine.*

   Miserere In classical Latin *misereri* is generally deponent. An active form appears as early as Ennius, rarely, and never in V.

   orationem Always 'prayer' in the Psalms.

4.3 **Filii hominum** More literally, *filii viri* = bᵉnê ʾîš . The Hebrew phrase designates people of wealth and prominence or, by another interpretation, highlights their mortal status.

   usquequo gravi corde Supply *estis* or *eritis*. For the omission of the verb 'to be' see on 1.2 *voluntas. usquequo* ('how long') for *quousque* is perhaps influenced by the order of the underlying Greek and Hebrew words which = literally, 'unto what'. *Gravi corde* is ablative of description. Not 'heavy-hearted' but 'hardhearted, intransigent'. Cf. Exodus 8.32, *et ingravatum est cor Pharaonis*, 'And the heart of Pharaoh was hardened'.

Ut quid = *quare*. Occurs twice in Cicero but becomes common in ecclesiastical Latin under the influence of Greek and Hebrew idiom as a literal equivalent for ἵνα τί and **lammāh**.

4.4   **scitote quoniam** 'know that'. In later Latin *quoniam, quia, quod* followed by the indicative or subjunctive often replace the classical accusative and infinitive in indirect statement. In the Psalter the classical construction is rare.

4.5   **Irascimini** Possibly 'be angry (with yourselves)', that is, 'repent'. The Hebrew verb is more general and means 'tremble' whether in joy, sorrow, anger, or awe.

quae dicitis in cordibus vestris In Hebrew, 'to say in the heart' = 'think, ponder'.

quae dicitis in cordibus vestris in cubilibus vestris conpungimini 'feel remorse for what you say in your hearts', a possible translation of LXX, but more likely the Greek verb here = 'keep quiet'. *in cordibus vestris in cubilibus vestris* describes the locale of private thoughts.

4.6   **sacrificium iustitiae** 'a sacrifice of justice', that is 'a just, acceptable sacrifice'.

Quis ostendet nobis bona Following the literal translation of the LXX. The Hebrew question is actually the idiomatic equivalent of an *utinam* clause: *Utinam bona ostendantur nobis*. In Christian exegesis, by a sort of *idioma scripturae*, *quis* is taken to imply 'there is no one' or 'there is scarcely anyone'.

4.7   **Signatum est super nos lumen vultus tui** To Augustine, the well-known *Nummi Dei sumus* metaphor, inspired in part by Genesis 1.26 and referring to minting in which the picture of a ruler is impressed upon coins. 'For man was made in the image and likeness of God which he defaced by sinning.'

4.8   **A fructu frumenti et vini et olei sui multiplicati sunt** V is scarcely intelligible here since it follows LXX's slavish and possibly corrupt rendering of a highly elliptical Hebrew original: 'You have put joy in my heart more than at the time (when) their grain and new wine abound.' In LXX ἀπὸ καιροῦ ('more than time') was corrupted to ἀπὸ καρποῦ ('more than fruit'). The 'sentence' is to be closely joined to what precedes. 'You have put joy in my heart more than (the joy from) the fruit of their grain and wine and oil (with which) they have been enriched.' For *a* = 'more than' (Hebrew comparative particle min, 'from') cf. 72.25 *a te quid volui super terram*, 'what more than You do I desire upon the earth'. The parataxis and omission of a relative after *sui* is quite clumsy. Augustine would take *sui* = 'of Him (God)'; thus, 'from the time of His grain'. In V the reflexive adjective is sometimes used for *eius, eorum* and vice versa. Jer.'s *eorum* for *sui* simply excises the difficulty. Note also that Augustine's text has *tempore* for *fructu*. The Latin would be more naturally interpreted as 'they (the *multi* or men in general) have been enriched by (*a = propter*) the fruit of their grain ...'. In either case, the basic contrast is between the speaker's divinely inspired joy and the joy of the others that comes from temporal things.

4.9   **In pace** 'peacefully'.

in id ipsum 'in the selfsame', i.e. 'together, at the same time'. The Hebrew is clearer: 'As soon as I lie down, I go to sleep in peace', an expression of the psalmist's absolute confidence in God. *ipse = idem* is common in V probably from the confusion of ὁ αὐτός, 'the same one' and αὐτός ὁ, 'he himself'. In general, however, *ipse = idem* is well attested in later Latin. Augustine remarks on the future tense of the verbs and interprets the statement as referring to the future peaceful repose of the blessed.

4.10   **Quoniam tu Domine singulariter in spe constituisti me** Either 'since You Lord singly (alone) have established me in security' or 'since You Lord have established me separately (apart) in security'. The second translation is sometimes justified by Deuteronomy 33.28: *habitabit Israhel confidenter et solus*. Augustine is closer to the second translation since he interprets *singulariter* as contrastive to *multi* of 4.6

Psalm 5

Again, originally an individual lament.

5.1   **In finem** See on 4.1 *in finem.*

pro ea quae hereditatem consequitur The Latin follows closely the Greek's misinterpretation of the Hebrew. A difficult, technical term, the Hebrew phrase perhaps gives musical directions:

'for flute accompaniment'. Augustine and Bede, among other Christian exegetes, interpreted the Latin allegorically and detected reference to the church, *Ecclesia*: 'on behalf of Her who acquires the (divine) inheritance'. To them, the Church is speaking here.

Psalmus David Mention of the *templum* in verse 8 historically precludes David's authorship.

5.2   **auribus percipe** 'give ear to'. The verb occurs only in the imperative in the Psalter.

intellege Perhaps not 'understand', but 'pay attention to, attend to', in view of the parallelism to the preceding and following petitions.

clamorem 'cry of pain, lamentation'.

5.3   **Intende** 'pay attention to'.

voci orationis meae Literally, 'the sound of my prayer', but the Hebrew is better translated 'my suppliant voice' or 'my cry for help'. The second noun, like an adjective, actually qualifies the first. Cf. 4.2, *Deus iustitiae meae*: 'voice of prayer' = 'prayerful, suppliant voice'.

5.4   **Quoniam ad te** 'since (it is) to You'. Note the emphatic position of *ad te.*

orabo The future.

5.5   **adstabo** 'I shall stand by, wait', or simply 'I shall stand in the presence of'. The Hebrew is literally, 'I shall stretch out for You' (or perhaps, 'prepare') and commentators supply various direct objects: 'my requests, my case, my sacrifice'.

videbo 'I shall watch, keep watch (for your answer)', a post-classical meaning.

quoniam The clause is better construed as independent of the preceding. 'For You are ...' *quoniam* = *enim* is common in V.

volens 'who delights in'. The participle in place of the relative clause reflects the Greek participle.

5.6   **ante oculos tuos** See on 3.1. *a facie.*

5.7   **Odisti** In V *odi* is conjugated as though from *odire.* syncopated

operantur 'work, do'. A common word in ecclesiastical Latin with a variety of meanings: 'carry into effect, cause, administer, do good works'.

iniquitatem = *inique*. An abstract noun with *operari* often virtually equals an adverb.

Virum sanguinum The phrase literally reproduces the Hebrew construct chain even to duplicating the plural of composition *sanguinum:* literally, 'a man (of pools) of blood', i.e. 'a bloodthirsty man'. In Hebrew, blood in the body is singular but blood that has been shed is plural.

5.8   **in multitudine misericordiae tuae** Another Hebraism, 'in the abundance of Your mercy'.

adorabo ad Either 'I shall worship toward (near)' or 'I shall approach (as a worshipper) toward'.

in timore tuo A modal phrase expressing the manner of worship or approach: 'with respect for you'.

5.9   **deduc me in iustitia tua** 'guide me in (the path of) Your justice' or 'guide me in (view of) Your justice', i.e. for the sake of Your justice.

propter inimicos meos Literally, 'on account of my enemies', i.e. since they exist and affront Your *iustitia*.

dirige in conspectu meo viam tuam Since *meo* and *tuam* feel reversed, most scholars regard the text as corrupted from *dirige in conspectu tuo viam meam*, but the sense is similar: 'make straight your (just) way in my sight', and perhaps deliberately parallel to '*deduc me ...*'.

5.11   **iudica** 'Pronounce sentence upon, condemn'.

Decidant a cogitationibus suis Probably 'let them fall by (*a = propter*) their own evil designs'.

secundum multitudinem impietatum eorum 'because of their many impieties', but to Augustine, quantitative: 'in proportion to their many impieties' drive them away, i.e. drive them far away.

5.13   **benedices iusto** The accusative and dative both occur with *benedicere* in V. For *benedicere* in the opposite sense 'say farewell to, renounce, curse', cf. Job 2.9 *benedic Deo et morere*.

ut scuto 'as with a shield'. The Hebrew word signifies a shield that covers the entire body.

coronasti 'You have surrounded'. The peculiar juxtaposition of *coronare* (properly, 'to crown') and *scutum* may be due to a lacuna in the Hebrew text. Also the Hebrew verb form may be pointed to mean either 'surround' or 'crown'.

Psalm 6

Originally an individual lament, but later the first of the seven so-called Penitential Psalms (6, 31, 37, 50, 101, 129, 142) perhaps so classified in the time of Augustine though the first explicit reference is in Cassiodorus (*c.* 485-580). Whether consciousness of guilt was a dominant theme in the Hebrew is debateable. In the later Church, each Psalm was regarded as one of seven steps on the ladder of repentance. Because its theme is contriteness arising merely from fear of punishment, 6 was taken as the first. To Augustine, the Church is again the speaker here.

6.1   **pro octava** Literally, 'for the eighth'. The precise meaning of the heading in Hebrew is obscure. Perhaps it gives directions for musical accompaniment: 'on the 8-stringed instrument'. In Christian interpretation it was regarded as a reference to the age of perpetual bliss after the seventh age of judgement or to the final day of judgement after the work of the world is finished in seven 'days'.

6.2   **ne ... corripias me** Note the parallelism in the couplet. The construction *ne* with present subjunctive is usually avoided in Ciceronian Latin perhaps to prevent confusion with a final clause.

     furore ... ira The word for anger in the second place in Hebrew is actually better translated '*furor*' since it implies 'hot displeasure'. Later exegetes often sought to distinguish the two: e.g. Petrus Chrysologus: *Ira Dei est delinquentium poena, furor Dei est supplicium peccatorum,* or Albertus Magnus' notion of *ira* alluding to punishment in purgatory, *furor*, punishment in Hell.

6.3   **infirmus** The Hebrew may have originally referred to a physical affliction or the language may be metaphorical.

     conturbata sunt For Hebrew 'are in agony'. The flatness of the Latin results from LXX's tendency to overuse ταράσσω ('trouble') to translate many different Hebrew verbs (16, for example in the Psalter alone). Note below: 6.3 *turbata est*; 6.8 *turbatus est.*

6.4   **usquequo** For the more usual *quousque*. The order is perhaps influenced by LXX ἕως πότε, literally, 'until when', which in turn closely follows the Hebrew order.

6.5   **Convertere** Present imperative passive with a medial or reflexive sense: 'turn (yourself)'. Understand *ad me*, 'toward me'.

     animam meam In the Hebrew = 'my life'.

6.6   **inferno** Hebrew 'Sheol' a designation of the netherworld, quite different from the Christian reading of the word as designating place of eternal punishment, Hell.

     quis See on *quis ostendet nobis bona,* 4.6.

confitebitur *confiteor* in Christian Latin either = 'acknowledge one's sins, confess' or 'praise' as here. The first meaning derives from the Latin tradition, the second from the Greek and Hebrew.

6.7   **Laboravi in gemitu meo** 'I am worn out by my groaning'.

lavabo ... rigabo The futures reflect Hebrew imperfects, the first of which is more forceful: 'I flood ... and drench'.

per singulas noctes 'every night' *per* here implies repetition; cf. Luke 2.41, *per omnes annos* = 'every year'.

6.8   **Turbatus est** See above 6.3, *conturbata est*. Hebrew, 'wastes away'.

a furore After LXX's ἀπὸ θυμοῦ. *a* = *propter*. In this context the Hebrew word is probably better rendered 'grief' than 'anger'. The LXX translators often use θυμός for any strong emotion and V simply equates θυμός to *furor*, sometimes inappropriately.

inveteravi 'grow old, fail in strength'. Follows LXX but in MT 'eye' is still subject.

inter Translates Greek ἐν which reflects Hebrew bᵉ which here is probably not local but causal = *propter*.

6.10   **Exaudivit** 'has listened to, granted'. The verb is similarly used by Roman writers in relation to the gods.

deprecationem Properly 'a prayer for pardon'.

6.11   **convertantur** To Augustine a reference to conversion and repentance. The Hebrew means no more than 'they shall turn back'.

Psalm 7

7.1   **Psalmus** In the Hebrew text the word is **shiggaion**. Found only here in the Psalter, it perhaps means more specifically a Psalm of lamentation though the Psalm itself contains several different elements.

pro verbis Chusi filii Iemini 'because (*pro* = *propter* [cf. French *pour*]) of the words of Cush, the Benjaminite'. Hebrew **bēn** = *filius*. Apparent allusion to some incident of Benjaminite opposition to and possibly slander of David. The identity of Cush is uncertain. In later Jewish Talmudic tradition he is identified as Saul. Note, in Hebrew, 'words' may also = 'things, matters'. **Chusi** is not a marked genitive but an indeclinable, deriving from the LXX's transliteration, Χουσι.

7.2   **speravi** Hebrew 'I have taken refuge'.

persequentibus 'those who pursue', a substantival participle which reflects Greek and Hebrew idiom but which is not unidiomatic Latin. Cf. 3.4 *exaltans caput meum.*

7.3   **Nequando** Occurs frequently in the Psalter as a useful literal equivalent of LXX's Greek μήποτε, 'that not at any time'.

rapiat The shift in number from plural indefinite *persequentibus* to singular 'he' = 'one' = 'they' is not impossible in the Hebrew. Since it would be odd in Latin, Augustine interpreted the shift as a reference to the Adversary of the soul, the Devil.

leo The Asiatic lion, now extinct.

animam meam In Hebrew, a periphrasis for 'me'. See on *animae meae*, 3.3.

non est qui redimat A relative clause after a assertion of non-existence usually takes the subjunctive. Translate: 'there is no one to ...'.

7.4   **istud** Probably refers to the accusation, unspecified in the text. In classical Latin *iste* is often used by a prosecutor to refer to a defendant. To Augustine the pronoun either stands for sin in general or refers to what immediately follows.

7.5   **si reddidi retribuentibus mihi mala** *mala* may be construed with both verbs: 'If I have paid back evils to those giving me evils' (*retribuo = tribuo*); or only with *reddidi*: 'If I have paid back evils to those giving back duly to me'. The second rendering is closer to the Hebrew: 'If I have done wrong to my friend.'

7.6   **conculcet** 'may he trample'.

in terra = *in terram.*

7.7   **in finibus inimicorum meorum** 'in the territories of my enemies'. The Hebrew has 'against the excessive fury of my enemies'. The LXX apparently confused two similarly spelled Hebrew words, one for 'limits, boundaries', the other for 'anger'. V follows the mistranslation.

in praecepto quod mandasti 'according to the order which You have commanded'. The psalmist seemingly speaks as though God had already issued an order for judgement. The translator has in fact misunderstood the Hebrew precative perfect used in prayer where the speaker is expressing a confident wish. Cf. the proper NIV translation: 'decree justice', literally, 'for me You have appointed a judgement'.

7.8   **synagoga** The Latin preserves the Greek word here, such transliteration being a tendency of the Old Latin versions. In Jer. the word occurs only once, notably to refer to the group of Jews who rebelled against Moses and God (Ps. 105). *Coetus, congregatio* would have been better renderings.

propter hanc 'for the sake of this assembly'. The Hebrew may mean 'above it', i.e. the assembly. Alternatively, *hanc* is sometimes taken as a Hebraizing feminine for neuter = *hoc*.

in altum 'on high', an appropriate location from which to dispense justice.

regredere The original Hebrew verb might have been 'be enthroned'. Augustine interprets the returning on high as Christ's ascension after which the Holy Spirit was dispatched to assist those preaching the Gospel.

7.9 **super me** 'which is in me'. *super* often crudely reproduces Greek ἐπί which has a range of meanings wider than the Latin preposition. Augustine takes the phrase literally, 'that is upon me' and refers to both *iustitiam* and *innocentiam* which, coming from God, light the soul. As the candle is judged not of itself but by the flame upon it, the soul is to be judged not of itself, but by qualities kindled upon it by God.

7.10 **diriges** 'to set aright, stabilize'.

corda et renes 'hearts and kidneys', the organs respectively of intelligence and emotions, English 'minds and hearts'. The phrase suggests a more insightful judgement than any terrestrial judge could execute. In additon to inmost thoughts, in Christian exegesis the kidneys are also sometimes associated with concupiscence.

7.11 **Iustum adiutorium meum a Deo** 'rightful is the assistance to me from the Lord'. Follows the LXX which as usual, eliminates the Hebrew metonymy: 'a shield upon me is God' or perhaps 'my shield is with God'. The Hebrew text is problematic.

7.12 **numquid** Translates LXX's μή, but here completely alters the Hebrew's positive assertion of God's daily anger to a denying question: 'Surely God is not angry ...'. The question becomes a virtual expansion of *patiens*.

7.13 **gladium suum** In Hebrew the subject is not clear, God or the evil man; here, it is God.

vibrabit 'He will brandish His sword'.

7.14 **in eo** 'on it', i.e. the bow. The Hebrew may mean 'for him', i.e. 'for himself'. The malicious persecution of the enemy rebounds upon himself.

vasa mortis 'implements of death', i.e. 'deadly weapons'. The phrase is modelled on a Hebrew construct chain.

sagittas suas ardentibus effecit The Latin might be rendered 'he has made His arrows to (the disadvantage of) those burning (with anger)', i.e. the enemies of the speaker. Many interpreters, without explanation take *ardentibus* as = *ardentes* and so modifying *sagittas*. The dative ultimately reflects the Hebrew which may be translated 'He has made His arrows for (into) burning ones', i.e. 'as burning ones'.

7.16   **Lacum** 'open pit'. In the Vulgate Old Testament, *lacus* never has the classical meaning 'lake'.

7.17   **dolor eius** 'The anguish that he causes'. Subjective genitive.

7.18   **Confitebor** 'I will praise'. The future reflects the Hebrew emphatic imperfect or cohortative which expresses a strong desire on the speaker's part.

altissimi Translates the Hebrew epithet ʿelyon, the 'most High'.

Psalm 8

Originally a hymn of praise that focuses on the creation. In the services of the Catholic Church, the Psalm was used in the baptism of adults who were transformed from sons of Adam to infants of God.

8.1   **pro torcularibus** Literally, 'according to the winepresses', following the Greek translation of the obscure Hebrew original. Whether the Hebrew heading in fact meant 'Song of the Winepress' and referred to a setting or ceremony or actually indicated a musical instrument (Gittite lyre) is unknown. One Christian interpretation viewed the phrase as = *pro Gethaeis* = *Philistaeis* (Gath being a Philistine city) = *Gentilibus*, 'on behalf of the gentiles', a reference to their future conversion. Augustine related it variously to the Church, the Divine word, and martyrdoms.

8.2   **Quoniam** 'since' and so the causal clause is linked to the preceding exclamation. *Quoniam* = LXX's ὅτι = Hebrew relative marker, but the Hebrew text is corrupt and subject to conjecture; hence its many differing translations; e.g. NIV: 'You who have set your glory above the heavens', which translation simply omits the relative.

caelos This confusion of masculine and neuter genders occurs in the earliest Latin literature. Perhaps even before the first century BC, 'm' became silent at the end of polysyllables; hence certain nouns, regularly neuter in classical Latin, appear as masculines: *caelus, vinus, fatus.* The tendency was accelerated at the expense of the neuter; hence the nearly virtual disappearance of the neuter in Romance languages.

8.3   **perfecisti laudem** 'You have firmly established praise'. The Hebrew 'You have established a bulwark' or 'You have built up strength' sharpens the reference to 'infants' and 'sucklings', usually symbols of weakness.

inimicum et ultorem   Perhaps the twofold designation to parallel *infantes* and *lactantes.* From an Old Testament perspective the imagery of this entire verse is unique and difficult; to a Christian it is deceptively intelligible from its citation at Matthew 21.16.

8.4   **Quoniam** Reproduces LXX's ὅτι a mistranslation of Hebrew kî which here is temporal not causal; *quoniam* and *quomodo* in later Latin, however, do sometimes = 'when'. The temporal clause is subordinate to verse 5.

8.5   **Quid ... quod** The corresponding Hebrew pronoun and particle express a so-called abasement pattern, 'what is man that ...', a rhetorical question followed by a result clause. *quod* reproduced Greek ὅτι which in turn translates Hebrew kî.

filius hominis From a Hebrew perspective, merely a poetical synonym for *homo* which emphasizes mortality, but in Christian exegesis both it and the following *eum* are referred to Christ. In NT the phrase occurs 82 times to refer to Christ. To Augustine *homo* is 'earthly man', *filius hominis*, 'heavenly man', who follows Christ's example. Cf. *filii hominum*, 4.3.

visitas 'visit', either to punish or, as here, 'show concern for'.

8.6   **Minuisti eum paulo minus ab angelis** *ab* (= Hebrew particle min) expresses comparison: 'You have made him a little less than the angels'. Hebrew ˀĕlōhîm may = heavenly beings or God. *Angeli* follows LXX's but also probably correct interpretation. To Paul and Augustine, a reference to Christ and His humiliation in the Passion. Jerome also sees a Christological reference here and so translates the phrase *a deo* in Jer.

8.8   **pecora campi** 'beasts of the field', the undomesticated, wild animals as compared with *oves* and *boves.* For the genitives *campi, caeli, maris,* cf. 4.6 *sacrificium iustitiae.*

8.9 **qui perambulant semitas maris** Here to be construed with *pisces*. The Hebrew is ambiguous and may refer to a third class of creatures such as the *cete grandia* of Genesis 1:21. *Ambulare* is often used in later Latin as a virtual synonym of *ire*, but the translation 'roam about' works well here.

Psalm 9

The LXX combined two originally separate Hebrew Psalms (9-10) into one (9); hence, Vulgate Psalm 9 = Hebrew Psalms 9-10. The separate Psalms differed in type but were slightly altered and united in transmission. Thus the type that emerges is complex. Elements of thanksgiving and individual lament occur in 9.

9.1 **pro occultis filii** V follows LXX's probably unreliable translation of the Hebrew, the precise meaning of which is itself uncertain. Perhaps it originally furnished directions for the tune to which the Psalm was to be sung. Some Christian interpreters took the phrase to mean 'for the hidden things of the Son', a reference to the passion and death of Christ. Augustine understands *occultis* as the first advent of Christ which the Jews did not comprehend.

9.2 **Confitebor** Here 'I shall give thanks, praise', not 'I shall confess'. The future reflects the Hebrew imperfect which here has cohortative force.

in toto corde meo 'with my whole heart, sincerely'. The phrase expresses manner.

9.4 **In convertendo inimicum meum retrorsum** Reproduces the LXX's close rendition of a Hebrew circumstantial clause introduced by the preposition b^e, 'in'. Translate 'when my enemy is turned back ...'.

infirmabuntur et peribunt The shift from singular to plural is unidiomatic in Latin. Augustine accordingly takes *inimicum* in its usual Christian signification = 'Satan' and 'they' as *iniqui et impii*, but *inimicum* may simply be a collective singular.

9.5 **fecisti iudicium meum et causam meam** *iudicium facere* would normally mean 'pass judgement', but note *meum*. The phrase = Hebrew 'You have maintained (upheld) my right and my cause' (i.e. 'my just cause').

iudicium ... causam In Hebrew an emphatic repetition.

iudicas iustitiam The cognate accusative = *iuste*.

9.6   **impius** Collective singular.

in saeculum saeculi Literally, 'unto (future) time of (future) time', i.e. 'forever and ever'.

9.7   **defecerunt** 'have failed', in the sense 'give out' or 'become extinct'.

frameae In Tacitus, *framea* refers to a spear used by the Germans but in later Latin often signifies a sword, which is one way of reading the Hebrew here. The Greek word ῥομφαῖαι shows exactly the same semantic shift. *frameae* may be construed as the subject of defecerunt; *inimici*, as genitive dependent upon *frameae*. The Hebrew text may also be vocalized thus: 'The enemy are overtaken, ruins to endlessness', hence NIV: 'Endless ruin has overtaken the enemy'.

in finem The phrase expresses either manner, 'utterly' or time, 'forever'.

civitates 'the cities'.

cum sonitu Possibly 'with a crash'. The Latin follows the LXX which here departs from the Hebrew text, itself uncertain. An emphatic independent personal pronoun was probably misunderstood. Cf. Jer. *cum ipsis*.

9.8   **Et** Follows LXX's too literal translation of Hebrew 'and' which here is contrastive = autem.

in iudicio 'for judgement', i.e. 'to conduct judgement'. *In* with the ablative, in V, is sometimes used to express purpose as though = *ad* with the accusative. Underlying the construction is the flexible Hebrew preposition l^{e}.

9.10   **pauperi** Jer's *oppresso* is closer to the Hebrew.

in oportunitatibus in tribulatione Literally, 'at critical moments in tribulation', after the LXX ἐν εὐκαιρίαις ἐν θλίψει. ἐν θλίψει and so *in tribulatione* is the result of vocalizing the Hebrew text b^{e} ṣarah ('in trouble') rather than baṣṣarah ('distress'), i.e. 'in times of distress'.

9.11   **quaerentes** The substantival participle.

9.12   **studia eius** The Hebrew word is often used of God's 'works' and more specifically His wondrous works on behalf of His people. Hence, *studia* may = not merely 'pursuits, activities', but 'devoted actions' or even 'energetic attentions' on behalf of His people.

9.13   **requirens sanguinem** 'He who seeks blood', i.e. God. *requirere* in this context more exactly = 'avenge'. Here Greek idiom is reflected since in classical Latin the substantival participle usually occurs in cases other than the nominative.

eorum The accusative with *recordor*, 'be mindful of', is more common in classical Latin.

9.14 **humilitatem** Not 'humility' as commonly in ecclesiastical Latin, but 'low condition, degradation'.

de inimicis meis 'from my enemies', i.e. 'caused by my enemies'. *de* reflects the Hebrew preposition **min** which here expresses agency.

9.15 **in portis** In Jewish cities a place of assembly like the Greek agora or Roman *forum*.

filiae Sion A poetic way of referring to the people of Jerusalem or to the 'mother' city herself.

9.16 **salutari** 'help, salvation'. The adjective *salutaris* used as a noun instead of *salus* reflects the LXX's use of the adjective σωτήριος in place of σωτηρία.

fecerunt Supply *mihi*.

In laqueo The imagery is drawn from hunting.

9.17 **iudicia faciens** Imitates the Greek circumstantial participle which here expresses means: 'through the judgements he makes'.

Canticum = Hebrew **higgaion** (meditation), a notation indicating a soft meditative mood for the musical accompaniment. For *diapsalmatis* (= Hebrew **selāh**) see on *diapsalma*, 2.2.

9.18 **infernum** See on 6.6, *inferno*.

9.20 **confortetur** A late Latin word, *confortare* in the passive means here, in a positive sense, 'to be much strengthened, to prevail'. Elsewhere, in a negative sense, 'to be overbearing'.

Homo 'mere man'.

9.21 **Constitue ... legislatorem** V follows LXX. MT suggests the translation *incute terrorem*. Confusion may have arisen because of the similar form of the Hebrew words for teacher, lawgiver and fear.

quoniam homines sunt 'that they are (mere) human beings'. *Quoniam*, like Greek ὅτι, introduces a dependent statement after a verb of knowing.

9.22 (1) The second half of Ps. 9 in V and LXX, but Ps. 10 in the MT. A frequently obscure selection since it so closely reproduces the LXX's literal translation of a difficult Hebrew text which often seems to depart from MT.

Ut quid Domine For *ut quid = quare*, see on 4.3.

dispicis Translates the Greek ὑπερορᾳ̂ς from ὑπερορἀω, 'overlook, despise'. The Hebrew has 'do You hide Yourself', an anthropomorphism which the LXX translators typically altered out of respect.

in oportunitatibus in tribulatione See on 9.10.

9.23 (2) Dum superbit impius incenditur pauper Literally, 'while the impious is arrogant, the poor man is set on fire', i.e. the poor man is consumed by the arrogance of the impious. Cf. Jer. *in superbia impii ardet pauper*. In later exegesis burning is sometimes interpreted positively as movement toward greater purity as gold is refined in a furnace.

conprehenduntur in consiliis quibus cogitant From the Latin, at least three meanings are possible. (1) The impious are caught in their own intrigues. (2) The poor are caught in the plots of the impious. (3) The poor are overtaken in the midst of their own plans. The Hebrew imperfect here may be jussive = *comprehendantur*, which would support (1).

in consiliis quibus = *in consiliis quae.* A crudely literal attempt to imitate the Greek construction by which a relative pronoun is attracted into the case of its antecedent.

9.24 (3) laudatur ... in 'praises himself in, congratulates himself on'. The Latin passive, which historically originated from an undifferentiated Indo-European medio-passive, here represents the Greek middle voice which sometimes has reflexive force. Augustine takes the verb as passive 'is praised'.

benedicitur Again, may be taken in a middle reflexive sense. Cf. however, Augustine, 'is blessed'.

9.25 (4) secundum multitudinem irae suae non quaeret Three translations of the Latin are possible: (1) 'In proportion to the magnitude of His anger, God will not seek (after me)', thus representing the overconfident words of the *peccator*. (2) 'Because of the magnitude of his anger the sinner will not seek God'. (3) 'Because of (i.e. blinded by) the magnitude of his anger, (the sinner thinks) God will not seek (after me)'. The Hebrew text is also ambiguous. Note, however, the parallel to interpretation (1) in verse 34(13) below, *non requiret.*

9.26 (5) Non est Deus in conspectu eius 'there is no God in his presence', i.e. 'in his thoughts'; in Hebrew, not atheism, but a lack of belief in God's effective presence.

inquinatae sunt Follows LXX's mistranslation. The Hebrew verb means 'are firmly established', thus 'are prosperous'. The Latin seems hardly consistent with what follows: *omnium inimicorum suorum dominabitur*. The sinner's present successes, in fact transitory, inspire his arrogance. The inadequate translation of tenses also garbles the sense. As it stands, *inquinatae sunt* may be taken as a consequence of *non est Deus in conspectu eius.*

in omni tempore 'at all times'.

Auferuntur iudicia tua a facie eius That is, he forgets the stern penalties You exact in judgement. For *a facie* = *a*, see on 3.1.

omnium inimicorum suorum dominabitur 'He will domineer over (cf. MT snort, puff at) all his enemies'. The genitive after *dominari* is a Grecism. In the classical period the construction is found in poets imitating Greek authors. The future again is an unidiomatic translation of the imperfect.

9.27(6) Dixit enim in corde suo In Hebrew 'to say in the heart' = 'to think'.

Non movebor a generatione in generationem i.e. I shall never be disturbed.

sine malo Supply *ero*. 'I shall be without evil', i.e. 'nothing bad will happen to me'. Augustine links the phrase to *movebor*, 'I shall not be moved from generation to generation without evildoing', i.e. 'I will not secure fame among posterity unless I do evil'.

9.28(7) sub lingua = *in lingua*, but in Hebrew the preposition perhaps refers to a prolonged savouring of evil 'under the tongue' or the preposition may express duplicity and concealment in accord with the imagery that follows.

9.29(8) cum divitibus The MT here reads 'in the villages'. The words 'rich' and 'villages' in Hebrew are spelled differently but pronounced nearly alike.

9.30(9) rapere The infinitive to express purpose, rare in classical prose but common in the V partly through the influence of post-classical Greek.

dum adtrahit eum 'while he draws him to (himself)'. The Hebrew connects with what follows, 'he seizes the poor man when he draws him into his net'.

9.31(10) inclinabit se et cadet The Latin is obscure as is the Hebrew original. The subject of *inclinabit* may be the evildoer ('he will bend himself' = crouch in waiting), the subject of *cadet* being the poor man; or the subject in both cases may be the poor man.

9.34(13) Non requiret 'He (God) will not demand satisfaction'.

9.35(14) Vides 'You (God) do see ...', the psalmist's emphatic and confident response to *non requiret*.

>**quoniam** 'since', but Hebrew kî here may be emphatic.

>**laborem et dolorem** 'the trouble and pain' caused by the impious.

>**eos** Either refers to *laborem et dolorem,* to take them in hand, deal with them (*eos* = Greek masculine αὐτούς) or refers to *impii*, to inflict punishment upon them.

>**Tibi derelictus est** *derelinquere* in a legal context = 'give up a claim to', hence, 'abandon'; here the force is perhaps middle: 'has put himself under Your care', or passive 'has been left to You'.

9.36(15) quaeretur peccatum illius et non invenietur In Hebrew, 'to seek and not find something' is a proverbial way of signifying that it has completely disappeared or perished. Thus, here, his sinful way shall disappear completely.

9.38(17) exaudivit Corresponding to the Hebrew perfect, which here is a sort of prophetic preterite since God has not yet acted. The use of this tense emphasizes the confident faith of the psalmist that God will in fact act in his behalf.

>**praeparationem cordis eorum** Whatever the heart prepares or makes ready; hence, its prayers and petitions.

9.39(18) iudicare An infinitive of purpose loosely joined to what precedes.

>**pupillo et humili** Instead of accusatives, datives of advantage reflecting the Greek: 'to give judgement in favour of ...'.

>**ut non adponat ... magnificare se homo** Literally, 'so that man may not add to (continue to) esteem himself highly'. The use of *adponere* to express repeated action is a Hebraism. The classical distinction between *ne* and *ut non* is often not preserved in V. The Hebrew is also translated 'so that man on earth will no longer cause terror'. *super terram* then would have to be construed as attributive = 'earthly', i.e. 'mere', not adverbial.

Psalm 10

Originally an individual lament, set forth, however, in a tone of confidence.

10.2 **quomodo dicitis** The tone of the question is indignant: 'How can you say ...'. The 'you' refers to the psalmist's advisors.

animae meae = *mihi*. See on 3.3 *animae meae*.

sicut In LXX (ὡς) but not in MT. Hebrew poetry does not require a particle of comparison

passer Translates LXX's στρουθίον, diminutive of στρουθός, 'sparrow'. The Hebrew word is less specific = *avis* and may be implicitly comparative (like a bird) or vocative.

10.3 **Quoniam** = *enim*.

ecce 'look!' The particle forcefully draws attention to the immediacy of the sinners' murderous actions.

intenderunt arcum 'have stretched the bow', but in Hebrew 'have stepped upon the bow' (to bend and string it).

in faretra Follows LXX but MT has 'upon the string'.

sagittent A late Latin word.

in obscuro 'in darkness'.

10.4 **Quoniam** In the Hebrew, the clause may be subordinate to the question that follows: 'When the foundations are broken down, what can the righteous man do?' Perhaps these are again the words of the psalmist's misguided advisors. Hebrew 'foundations' probably = the community's 'law and order'. LXX and V, however, may be translated 'for what You (God) have perfected, they have destroyed'. *Quoniam* may then also be taken as introducing an independent proposition since it sometimes = *enim* in V.

fecit The perfect tense here is obviously unidiomatic in Latin and simply reflects LXX's aorist. MT has the perfect which indicates the advisors' certitude of the futility of the just man's actions under these disastrous circumstances: 'what can the just man do?' Puzzled by the tense, Christian exegetes related the question to Christ: 'what has He, the just Man par excellence, done (to deserve such treatment)?' *Quae perficisti destruxerunt* then was taken to refer to the persecutors' destruction by crucifixion of the perfected Son (vague *quae* for *quem*), while all the sinners' murderous actions alluded to heresies within the Church. Altogether an excellent example of how V's retention of Hebrew idiom affected later exegesis.

10.5 **Dominus in caelo sedis eius** 'As to the Lord, His throne (is) in heaven'. Note *sedis* = *sedes,* nominative. The unattached nominative (here, *Dominus*) becomes fairly common in later Latin, but in V, Hebrew influence should not be ruled out.

in pauperem Collective singular.

palpebrae 'eyelids' but here virtually synonymous with *oculi*. In Hebrew, a poetical counterbalance.

10.6 **odit animam suam** The subject is *qui diligit iniquitatem*, but in MT 'His soul' (= God) is the subject; perhaps a reverential alteration, after LXX, to avoid imputing hatred to God. The Latin reflexive translates LXX's ἑαυτοῦ, 'of himself' (Hebrew, simply 'of him').

10.7 **Pluet** The subject is personal, God.

laqueos 'nooses', a metaphor of death and destruction but the Hebrew word is perhaps better translated 'fiery coals'.

pars calicis eorum 'the portion of their cup' = 'their just reward'. At a banquet the head of the feast apportioned a certain amount to each guest; hence, the notion of what one gets or deserves.

10.8 **dilexit** The perfect translates the Greek aorist which represents the Hebrew perfect in a statement of general truth.

aequitatem 'righteousness', a common meaning in ecclesiastical Latin. The abstract is used for the concrete, 'the righteous'.

vidit The perfect reproduces the Greek aorist which here translates the Hebrew imperfect expressing a general truth. For the sentiment cf. 12.1 *usquequo avertis faciem tuam a me.*

Psalm 11

Originally a Psalm of lamentation, whether individual or communal.

11.2 **defecit** See on *defecerunt*, 9.7.

sanctus Collective singular (Hebrew ḥāsîd, the 'godly man' who follows the covenant and God's will).

veritates The plural reflects the Hebrew. In earlier Latin the plural = 'expressions of truth, truths'. Given the parallel with ḥāsîd the Hebrew is probably not abstract but = '(persons of) faithfulness', i.e. 'trustworthy persons'. Cf. Jer. *fideles*. In general in the Psalms the translation *veritas* obscures the meaning 'fidelity, faithfulness' behind which lies originally the relationship to the covenant. Historically, the extension of the classical meaning may be traced to the LXX's translation of Hebrew ꝰᵉmeṯ by ἀλήθεια. To Augustine the plural refers to the individual holy souls who are enlightened by God's unique 'Truth'.

parallelism gives it away

not grammatical, but makes sense

11.3   **Vana** 'falsehoods'.

construction ad sensum

←**unusquisque** More idiomatic Latin than the usual literal translation *vir. proximum suum* reflects the literal equivalent of a Hebrew reciprocal pronoun: '(to) one another'.

labia dolosa A so-called nominative absolute not grammatically connected to what follows. Its use here depends ultimately on the Hebrew since even the corresponding Greek accusative of respect (χείλη δόλια) strains idiom. Either supply *sunt* or connect as though it were as an ablative of means with *locuti sunt*.

in corde et corde 'with a heart and a heart', a literal translation of the Hebrew which means 'with a twofold heart, duplicitously'; so, Augustine, *duplex cor significat.* Repeated words joined by 'and' often express variety; *in*, like Hebrew b⁰, expresses modality or means.   *two-faced*

11.4   **magniloquam** 'boastful'.

11.5   **Linguam nostram magnificabimus** The precise meaning of the hiphil of the Hebrew root (**g-b-r** 'be strong') is not clear. One might naturally render the Latin 'we shall esteem greatly our tongue'. Cf. Augustine, 'Proud hypocrites are meant who rely on their speech to deceive men and do not submit to God'. *Magnificare* is also used in the V to express intensive or repeated action. The Hebrew might mean 'we shall prevail by our tongues', and it is possible to translate the Latin 'we shall show forth the power of our tongue'.

a nobis sunt *a nobis* = *a parte nostra*; hence, 'are on our side', or, alternatively, *a nobis sunt* = 'belong to us'.

quis noster dominus est The tone of the question is arrogant negative answer is expected. See on 4.6. *quis ostendet ... .*

11.6   **salutari** 'safety, security', but to Augustine = *Christo.*

reciprocity

fiducialiter agam in eo 'I shall act decisively in his (the poor man's) case'. The abrupt change to the singular number is not uncommon. The Latin reflects LXX, but the underlying Hebrew text is uncertain.

11.7   **probatum terrae** = LXX δοκίμον τῇ γῇ. *Terrae* is dative after LXX τῇ γῇ, 'tested in reference to the earth'. The Hebrew itself is obscure and variously emended. Jer.'s *probatum separatum a terra colatum septuplum* suggests that some phase of the smelting process is referred to, such as placing the molten metal in an earthen form 'in a furnace of clay'. It is difficult to draw this out of the Latin alone, however. Another possibility is: 'tested (approved) in the opinion of the world, universally approved', which is almost certainly not the original sense.

septuplum = classical *septies*, the usual number to denote perfection.

11.8	**a generatione hac et in aeternum** *a* probably expresses separation, not time from which. *et* then = 'even'; thus, the translation: 'separated from this generation even unto eternity'. To Augustine, the distinction is between this world, here, where we are needy and poor and the next world where we will be wealthy and rich.

11.9	**circuitu** In Hebrew simply 'round about' but to Augustine the *inclusio* 'cycle' of seven days which represents the impious' desire for temporal things; hence, they do not come to the eternal eighth.

spiritual ←**secundum altitudinem tuam multiplicasti filios hominum**

The Latin may be translated: 'in accordance with Your eminence You have multiplied the sons of men'. Both MT and LXX are of little use here, being obscure and corrupt; hence the difficulty of V. Some take 'sons of men' = 'the pious', but verse 2 suggests it = 'the wicked'. Thus, the Latin might also be translated: 'You have multiplied the sons of men (= the wicked) in accord with Your eminence', i.e. the flourishing of the wicked does not ultimately contradict Your sovereignty. 'Multiplication of the wicked' then closes the Psalm with an echo of the earlier 'extinction of the godly'. Technically, such closure is an *inclusio* .

Psalm 12

Again a Psalm of lament whether individual or communal. In Roman Catholic rite, this Psalm, like Psalm 3, came to be used in the rite of exorcism.

12.1	**In finem** Probably modal, 'utterly', but if a question mark is inserted after *Domine*, perhaps temporal, 'forever', expressing impatience. Augustine translates 'with respect to the End', i.e. Christ, as though God were delaying the speaker from understanding 'Christ, the Wisdom of God'. This translation obviously follows from the Christian interpretation of *in finem* in the Psalm's title. See on 4.1.

avertis faciem Normally a sign of divine displeasure or punishment.

12.2 **Quamdiu** The Hebrew, as if to heighten the desperate tone, repeats the introductory word for 'how long' four times. The LXX and V change the word in the third occurrence.

anima ponam consilia in mea V mechanically reproduces LXX θήσομαι βουλὰς ἐν ψυχῇ μου. The Hebrew word for 'plan', in some contexts, however, may be translated 'pain' and *dolores* was probably a better translation here, since normally *ponere consilium* = 'consult', which meaning is inconsistent with what follows: *dolorem* ... . Also, Hebrew nepeš (= *anima*) is normally a central organ of emotion, not intellectual activity.

per diem A probably too literal translation of Greek ἡμέρας. Hebrew yômām ('by day'), which here appears to = *per singulos dies, constanter*. Some Greek manuscripts preserve the reading 'day and night' which fits better but is probably for that reason a later correction. Perhaps sensing the oddness of the Latin, Augustine interprets *dies = tempus*, i.e. the temporal earthly existence.

12.3 **inimicus meus** Collective singular, but to Augustine, the Devil or carnal habit.

12.4 **Inlumina oculos meos** In Hebrew dimness of the eyes is a sign of loss of vitality or death; hence also a sign of the loss of God's blessing.

12.5 **motus fuero** The Hebrew is better translated 'fall' or 'be shaken'.

12.6 **Ego autem ... altissimi** Either the mood shifts abruptly or these lines are an expression of faith. In the first case *speravi* and *tribuit* refer to help already experienced. In the second case they reflect the Hebrew perfects which express confidence in a future event's occurrence.

et psallam ... altissimi Not in MT.

Psalm 13

The original genre is disputed but the Psalm contains elements of lament and wisdom.

13.1 **Dixit ... in corde suo** 'Because', remarks Augustine, 'no one dares to say this (*non est deus*) even if he has dared to think it.' The

Latin perfect is based on the Greek aorist of LXX which in turn reflects the Hebrew perfect. The Hebrew, however, expresses a general truth and is better translated in English as a present.

insipiens Collective singular. In Hebrew nābāl represents not an intellectual but a moral 'fool' who has shut himself off from God and His covenant.

Non est Deus In Latin the sentence is existential but from the Hebrew perspective it expresses a disbelief not in God but in His active, effective intervention in worldly affairs.

Corrupti sunt The subject now is *insipientes*, an abrupt change to the plural.

in studiis suis 'in their activities'. Cf. 9.12 *studia eius*.

non est qui faciat bonum Either continuing the thought of the previous verse or, originally, calculated hyperbole directed to the whole nation in danger of complete corruption.

non est usque ad unum Perhaps originally = 'he does not exist even to one', i.e. 'there is no one', but the Latin may also be construed, as Augustine observes, to mean 'no one exists except one'. To him the one, of course, is Christ.

13.2 **prospexit** The Hebrew perfect here would have been better translated as a present.

super filios hominum 'upon the sons of men', a broad designation if only the nation of Israel is meant.

si est intellegens 'if there is anyone having understanding'. Reflects a substantival participle in Hebrew and a participle without a definite article in Greek.

aut There is no disjunctive in the Hebrew; the participles may be appositional.

13.3 **Sepulchrum ... eorum** The verses do not occur in MT nor are they found in all the Greek manuscripts. Jerome pronounced them Christian interpolations derived from Paul, Romans 3.13-18, a passage which asserts that humankind in general is 'under sin' and which itself is modelled on parts of LXX Psalms 5, 9, 35, 139 and Isaiah.

Sepulchrum = *sepulcrum*. In V *c* or *ch* is used to transliterate Greek χ.

guttur 'throat'.

aspidum 'asps, poisonous serpents'.

Contritio 'destruction'.

81

13.4 **Nonne cognoscent** The future tense, to Augustine, threatens coming punishment.

qui operantur iniquitatem 'who do evil', the phrase is virtually a Hebrew calque.

qui devorat plebem meam sicut escam panis To Augustine, 'who devour my people like the food of bread' = 'who daily devour my people', since bread is a daily food. The underlying Hebrew text is difficult and subject to varying interpretations. Originally the contrast between eating bread which ultimately comes from God but not invoking God was probably mean to highlight the folly of the 'fools', but cf. NIV 'as men eat bread', which emphasizes the insatiateness of evildoers.

13.5 **illic** 'in those circumstances', namely, acts of evildoing, but the Hebrew adverb šām (usually = 'there') probably signals a momentous occurrence (= 'behold'?).

trepidaverunt timore 'they feared with a fear' = 'they feared greatly'. The ablative reflects the emphatic Hebrew cognate accusative.

ubi non erat timor The meaning of the Latin is not clear. Either (1) '(the evildoers) among whom there was no fear (of God) have feared greatly under those circumstances'; or (2) 'They feared greatly. Where did fear not exist?' thus emphasizing what precedes. In Augustine, they have feared greatly where there was no need to fear, i.e. for the loss of temporal things.

13.6 **Quoniam Deus in generatione iusta** sc. *est.* i.e. God is on the side of the righteous. *generatio* = Hebrew dôr which here perhaps is better translated 'assembly'.

consilium inopis confudistis quoniam Dominus spes eius est The Hebrew text is corrupt but perhaps means 'you evildoers frustrate the plans of the poor, but the Lord is their refuge' (NIV). As it stands, the Latin is = 'you have refuted (or shamed) the counsel of the poor man since (or *quoniam* = *quando* 'when') the Lord is his refuge'. Hebrew kî (= *quoniam*) here would have been better rendered *sed*. Augustine takes the verse as referring to the evildoers' disrespect for the lowly coming of Christ and setting their hopes in temporal things.

13.7 **Quis dabit ... salutare** The Latin follows the LXX's literal rendition of the Hebrew. In Hebrew the question is a way of expressing a wish or prayer and is better translated *utinam detur* *salutare.* In late Latin *salutare* is sometimes 'deliverance', as here, or 'saviour'. For the form of question, see on 4.6 *quis ostendet.*

Israhel Indeclinable indirect object of *dabit.*

averterit ... captivitatem A general deliverance is alluded to, not the Babylonian captivity.

exultabit Iacob et laetabitur Israhel The clauses are virtually synonymous, *Iacob = Israhel.* The names of the patriarch are used for the people of Israel.

Psalm 14

Perhaps originally an entrance liturgy recited as pilgrims sought entrance to the sanctuary on feast days. Wisdom traditon has broadened its purpose to a more general characterization of the righteous wise man.

14.1 **habitabit** The Hebrew denotes temporary residence or sojourn; hence *peregrinabitur* or *commorabitur* would be better here. The future represents the Hebrew imperfect of permission: 'who may dwell'.

tabernaculo 'tent' here probably an archaism for temple, but also recalls the tent in which Yahweh resided during the years of wandering.

Aut Apparently reflecting the Hebrew conjunction 'and' which occurs in some manuscripts. The two questions are parallel and virtually synonymous.

in monte sancto tuo Mount Zion.

14.2 **ingreditur** For walking as figurative of one's way of life, see on 1.1 *abiit. Ingredi* here = *ambulare.*

sine macula Hebrew tāmîn = *perfecte.*

operatur iustitiam 'works righeousness', i.e. does what is right, an ecclesiastical expression that is actually a Hebrew calque.

14.3 **in corde suo** i.e. sincerely. Internal and external behaviours are emphasized.

in lingua sua Expresses instrumentality.

obprobrium non accepit The Latin would naturally mean 'has not taken up reproach', i.e. has not gladly accepted malicious gossip, but *obprobrium accepit* (= LXX ὀνειδισμὸν ἔλαβεν) is simply a calque of Hebrew (ḥerpāh nāśāʾ) = 'lift up reproach, cast a slur'.

Ad nihilum deductus est 'is set at naught, is despised'.

14.4   **malignus** The 'evil man' whom God has rejected, contrasted with *timentes Dominum*.

iurat ... non decipit The Latin would mean simply that he keeps his oaths. In MT *proximo suo* by a slightly different reading is instead *ut se adfligat* as in Jer.; i.e., he keeps to his oath even if it hurts his interest.

14.5   **pecuniam suam non dedit ad usuram** i.e. 'has not lent his money at interest', a practice allowed only in dealings with non-Israelites.

munera 'gifts', i.e. 'bribes'.

super innocentes 'against innocent persons'.

non movebitur Often used to refer to the stable prosperity of the good person.

Psalm 15

This Psalm is sometimes classified as a song of confidence.

15.1   **Tituli inscriptio ipsi David** Sometimes translated 'a monumental inscription of David himself'. The Latin is based on LXX's στληγραφία, a rendering of Hebrew mıḵtām as though it were related to a root **k-t-m,** 'be indelible' or 'inscribe'?). In fact the exact meaning of mıḵtām is uncertain (possibly 'Psalm of atonement' or 'secret prayer'). For the possible meanings of *ipsi David* see note on *Psalmus David* 2.1. *Ipsi* represents the Greek definite article (τῷ Δαυείδ), i.e. it serves to mark the indeclinable name as dative.

15.2   **Dixi** MT has 'you have said', in the second person feminine singular form, but the form = *dixi* is found in some Hebrew manuscripts.

bonorum meorum non eges Literally, 'You have no need of my good things', i.e. 'You are not dependent on me'. The underlying Hebrew text may be corrupt and thus is variously emended and translated. Cf. Jer. *bene mihi non est sine te* which is perhaps closer to the original Hebrew.

15.3   **Sanctis ... mirificavit mihi: omnes voluntates meas in eis** In the Hebrew text *sanctis* may be taken as parallel to *Domino* and thus dependent on 'you have said' understood. Verses 2 and 3 then would represent the words of a syncretist who acknowledges both God and the so-called 'holy ones' (*sanctis* = g^{e}dōším = 'other deities'). *sanctis* here may be taken as loosely joined to *mirificavit* and anticipating *eis*: 'As for the pious ones ... He has wondrously fulfilled for me all my desires in them.' This translation strikes the colon from Weber's text.

15.4   **Multiplicatae sunt infirmitates eorum postea adceleraverunt** Literally, 'Their infirmities were increased. Afterwards they hastened.' Augustine, who regarded this Psalm as Messianic, understood *eorum* as referring to *sanctis*: The saints had their infirmities multiplied so that they might long for the Physician, Christ. After they were afflicted, they hastened to subject themselves to His care. The Latin is based ultimately on a faulty mistranslation of the Hebrew. The essential thought of the Hebrew appears to be: 'Let the sorrows of those increase who run after other gods.' In the Hebrew, the similar words for 'afterwards' and 'another (god)' may have been confused. *Post* may mean 'after' in the sense 'following, subjected to', *post carnem ambulant* 2 Peter 2:10, but to translate *postea adceleraverunt* 'They hastened after them' (*postea = post ea idola*) is rather abrupt.

   Non congregabo conventicula eorum de sanguinibus Literally, 'I shall not gather together their (small) assemblies from blood' which Augustine interprets as a reference to the saints' assemblies. It means, then, that the assemblies will not be carnal nor brought together by one propitiated by blood. The underlying Hebrew is difficult and possibly corrupt. The original reference may have been to participation in heathen sacrifices which involved shedding blood (human?). 'I shall not form their assemblies of blood', i.e. 'I shall not participate in their bloody assemblies'.

   nec memor ero nominum eorum per labia mea Again positively interpreted by Augustine: the Saints' former names are no longer important since they have been transmuted spiritually. In the Hebrew, the statement is an assertion to have no dealings with foreign gods, i.e. not to take their names upon one's lips.

15.5   **calicis mei** Cf. note on 10.7.

15.6   **Funes ceciderunt mihi in praeclaris** 'The (measuring) ropes have fallen for me in excellent places', an allusion to the ancient traditions of land allotment. In the sacral act of distributing land, the tribe of Levi was exempted since its means of livelihood derived from sacrifices and cultic payments. God was its share of the inheritance (verse 5); thus there may have been originally a reference to the Levitical status of the speaker, but this is perhaps too specific. Here the whole phrase is figurative and essentially parallel to and synonymous with *etenim hereditas mea praeclara est mihi.*

15.7 **insuper et usque ad noctem** Literally, 'above and even to the night'. The sense is 'ceaselessly'.

renes mei 'my kidneys', in Hebrew, organs of emotion; in English, we would say 'my heart'. Cf. 25.2.

15.8 **Providebam** Modelled on the Greek προορώμην which may have the local meaning 'see in front of one'. *providere* only rarely has this meaning, being usually temporal, 'see beforehand, foresee'. The Hebrew may refer to a theophany or an habitual keeping God before one, i.e. in one's mind.

15.9 **insuper ... (10) inferno** Perhaps originally these lines referred to some immediate danger of death facing the psalmist. As early as the Acts of the Apostles, however, they were taken as referring to Christ's resurrection.

caro mea 'my flesh, my body'. The Hebrew word often connotes frailty contrasted with the Deity.

in spe 'in (a state of) hope' or 'in (a feeling of) security'.

15.10 **videre** 'see' in the sense 'experience' after the Hebrew. *videre = pati* is another example of *idioma scripturae.*

corruptionem The Hebrew is not abstract but refers specifically to a pit in Sheol whose name may be interpreted in Greek as διαφθορά = *putredo* or *corruptio*. This LXX rendition facilitated the Christian use of the passage as a reference to Christ's resurrection.

vias vitae 'paths to life' perhaps originally meant no more than the paths to God not resurrection.

adimplebis 'You will fill'.

cum vultu tuo 'in association with Your divine face', i.e. in Your (divine) presence.

in dextera tua Parallel to *cum vultu tuo* and so locative not instrumental: 'at Your right hand'.

in finem Originally need not have meant 'forever' but simply 'to the end of a (long) life'.

Psalm 18

Sometimes classified as a wisdom hymn, Psalm 18 also contains elements of a hymn of creation.

18.1   **In finem** To Augustine this heading indicates that the Psalm relates to Christ.

18.2   **Caeli enarrant** The heavens are given voice by prosopopoeia. To Augustine the 'heavens' are the Evangelists in whom God dwells *tanquam in caelis*. Cf. the extended use of *caelum* in classical Latin to refer to 'the gods'. Also, in Hebrew the plural šāmayım may refer to the dwelling place or to the divine beings who serve God, the heavenly realm, but here is probably parallel to hārāgî[a][c] = *firmamentum*, 'the firmament'. The Latin preserves the chiasm: *caeli enarrant gloriam Dei* (ABC), *opera manuum eius adnuntiat firmamentum* (C'B'A').

Dei Translates Hebrew 'ēl. Note the transition to *Dominus* (Yahweh) in verses eight and following, evidence, to some scholars, that the Psalm is composed of two units, a hymn of creation (1-7) and a wisdom Psalm extolling *lex* = Torah (8-15).

opera manuum eius 'His handiwork'.

Firmamentum The plate above the earth that holds back the blue waters of the heavenly ocean.

18.3   **Dies diei eructat verbum et nox nocti indicat scientiam** In Hebrew the clauses are parallel expressions of the same conception: the continuity of the heavenly realm's proclamation. To Augustine *dies diei* refers to a direct spiritual transmission of knowledge about *Verbum* (Christ after John 1.1), while the second clause refers to the fleshly transmission of faith that brings future knowledge.

Eructat In classical Latin 'belches, vomits' but in Christian Latin often 'utters', used of the inspired language of the prophets. Here it reproduces Greek ἐρεύγεται which undergoes the same semantic shift ('belch, blurt out, utter'). The Hebrew verb yabbî[a][c]; also means 'to bubble forth' in ecstatic, spontaneous speech.

18.4   **Non sunt ... verba eorum** To Augustine verses 4 and 5 refer to the pervasiveness of missionary activity. Originally, however, they probably referred to nature's mysterious transmission of praise to God which is inaudible to uninitiated humans.

quorum ... eorum *eorum* is a superfluous Hebraism though the text of MT is slightly different here. In Hebrew the relative particle (here roughly = *quorum*) is not declined. Its syntactic relation to the antecedent is specified by an added, so-called resumptive pronoun (*eorum*).

18.6   **In sole** Perhaps originally a demythologizing of the sun as merely one of *opera manuum eius*. Verse 6 may have been a polemic against near Eastern and Egyptian notions of the sun as a god or bridegroom or a hero eager to run his course.

   gigans Reproduces Greek γίγας. The Hebrew may mean 'strong man, athlete, hero, warrior'.

18.7   **a summo caeli ... ad summum eius** 'from the one most remote end of heaven (the East) ... to its (other) end (the West)'. Cf. Augustine's slightly differing text and interpretation: *a summo caelo egressio eius* (= Christ's): *a patre egressio eius, non temporalis sed aeterna qua de Patre natus est.* The phrase *et occursus eius usque ad summum caeli* he then relates to Christ, in the fulness of His divinity, meeting the Father on an equal level.

   occursus *Circuitus* would have been a better translation.

18.8   **Lex Domini inmaculata** In the Hebrew, the 'Torah' but to Augustine the 'undefiled law' is Christ Himself 'who did not commit sin'. Like its Hebrew counterpart, *inmaculata* may be used in a sacrifical context of a victim 'without blemish', but here probably = *perfecta*, in the sense 'self-sufficient'.

   Domini *Domini* to *Dei* reproduces the Hebrew translation from 'ēl to Yahweh. The difference may reflect the separate origin of verses 8-15 or may be deliberately emphasizing the Lord as He reveals Himself to His people.

   convertens animas 'changing souls (for the better)'. In Hebrew, 'reviving souls', i.e. 'restoring life'. Augustine translates 'converting souls (to imitate Him in freedom)'. The participial construction reproduces the Greek which in turn imitates the Hebrew text.

   testimonium Not 'witness' but here parallel to and hence essentially synonymous with *lex* as is also *iustitia, preceptum*, and *iudicia*. For this meaning elsewhere in the Vulgate, cf. Ps. 118.157, *a testimoniis tuis non declinavi*, 'from Your ordinances ...' .

18.9   **lucidum** Hebrew bārāh 'radiant' and also 'pure'.

18.10   **Timor Domini** Would seem to spoil the parallelism with the synonyms of 'law' but 'fear of the Lord' here virtually = *religio Domini*; hence, His 'Law'.

18.11   **Desiderabilia super aurum** 'more desirable than gold'. Hebrew adjectives lack a comparative degree. To express comparison, the positive is used with mın ('relative to, from'); thus, the man is happier than I = the man is happy relative to me.

18.12   **retributio** A post-classical word which may mean 'retribution' or 'reward', as here.

18.13   **occultis** In the Hebrew, sins of which the sinner himself is not aware; e.g. unconscious cultic transgressions. To Augustine, the lusts which lie hidden within one.

18.14   **Et ab alienis parce tuo servo** A possible sense of the Latin is 'and preserve your servant from (the sins of) others', i.e. from their pernicious influence, but closer to LXX is 'and preserve from strangers (= foreign gods) your servant'. LXX apparently had zārîm (strangers) in its text while MT reads zēdîm 'presumptious ones (or sins)'.

   delicto maximo In Hebrew, probably idolatry; to Augustine, pride that commences with apostasy.

18.15   **Et erunt ut conplaceant eloquia oris mei** Literally, 'and the words of my mouth shall exist so that they be pleasing', i.e. shall be pleasing. The force of the underlying Hebrew imperfect is better given by simple *conplaceant*. The clumsy periphrasis follows LXX ἔσονται εἰς εὐδοκίαν which in turn follows literally the Hebrew: 'they shall be for satisfaction', i.e. be acceptable. εἰς εὐδοκίαν reflects a term for God's acceptance of sacrifice.

   adiutor Translates LXX βοηθέ, but MT = 'rock'.

Psalm 19

Perhaps originally a royal liturgy that began with the people's intercessory prayer for the king departing to battle.

19.2   **te Dominus** To Augustine, the Psalm prophetically relates to Christ's sacrificial suffering and death and their consequences. By this interpretation *te* = Christ, *Dominus* = God.

   in die tribulationis Originally alluding to the day of battle.

   nomen Dei In Hebrew, not merely a periphrasis for *Deus*, but a designation of the earthly *praesentia Dei*, His protective and efficacious power.

   Iacob The patriarch's name is used for the nation.

19.3   **de sancto** 'from His holy place', i.e. from Zion where the temple was located. In later Latin *de* gradually replaces both *ab* and *ex.* Thus in Romance languages the latter generally survive in prefixes.

19.4   **sacrificii** Hebrew minḥāh, in the post-Exilic period usually flour and oil. To Augustine this and *holocaustum* refer to Christ's sufferings in the Passion.

   holocaustum The offerings completely burnt upon the altar, no parts of which were returned to the worshippers.

   pingue fiat A conventional way of saying 'to prove acceptable to God' since fat was His special prerogative. Cf. Leviticus 3.16: *omne adipes Domini erit.*

19.6   **in ... magnificabimur** 'we shall be magnified in' after the LXX reading of the verbal root **(g-d-l,** 'be great'). MT has 'we shall set up our banners' **(d-g-l,** 'raise a banner').

19.7   **quoniam** To introduce indirect statement as usual in later Latin.

   salvum fecit In Hebrew, a perfect of certainty to express the psalmist's absolute confidence in God's future action.

   Christum suum See 2.2.

   in potentatibus salus dexterae eius 'by mighty deeds [is (or comes)] the salvation of His right hand', but in Hebrew 'by the mighty acts of salvation of His right hand', i.e. 'by the saving strength of His right hand'. *salutis* would have been more accurate than *salus*, and the singular *in potentia* (or *fortitudine*), a more idiomatic rendering of the intensifying Hebrew abstract plural.

19.8   **Hii ... hii** Supply *invocant*. The repeated use of the demonstrative is Hebraizing: 'some ... others'.

   in nomine ... invocabimus 'we shall make an invocation by means of the name'. The peculiar Latin reflects LXX tradition which is probably a calque of the Hebrew bᵉšēm ... nazkîr which may mean 'we shall boast of' or 'we shall swear by the name of', a way of saying 'we shall trust in the name of'. The difficulty is manifested by the various readings in the LXX and V. Cf. Augustine's text, *in nomine exsultabimus* which reflects another LXX tradition.

19.9   **obligati sunt** From obligare, 'to bind, entangle'. This perfect and the three that follow are all perfects of certainly which again express the psalmist's confidence.

Psalm 22

An important Psalm in early Christianity since it was viewed as prefiguring the sacraments of Baptism (water), the Eucharist (table, chalice), and Confirmation (oil). Originally perhaps a Psalm of confidence.

22.1 **Dominus reget me** 'The Lord will guide me, will direct my course'. *regere* may be used of directing animals but *pascere* would better have preserved the vivid shepherd metaphor of the Hebrew and Greek.

et Connects paratactically but the sense is 'since the Lord guides me, nothing will be wanting to me'.

22.2 **In loco pascuae** Literally, 'in a place of pasture-land'.

conlocavit *conloco*, 'put in'.

Super Follows LXX's ἐπί which reproduces Hebrew ʾal 'over the water' since probably not natural streams but artificial channels or containers of some kind are meant.

aquam refectionis 'water of refreshment', i.e. 'refreshing water'. See on. 4.2, *Deus iustitiae meae*. To Augustine and others, a reference to the waters of baptism.

22.3 **Animam meam convertit** Hebrew nepeš, which lies behind *animam* here probably means 'life' or, with the suffix pronoun, is simply a periphrasis for 'me'. 'He restores my life, he revives me.' A Christian might detect a reference to the spiritual 'soul'.

semitas iustitiae Literally, 'paths of righteousness', referring to a righteous course of life. This translation makes explicit the implicit moral figure in the Hebrew – 'right tracks, proper paths'. For the figurative use of *semita*, cf. 1.1 on *abiit*. For noun as adjective see on 4.2 *deus iustitiae*.

propter nomen suum Literally, 'on account of His name', i.e. in view of his reputation (for faithfulness to His flock) or 'for the glory of His name'.

22.4 **in medio umbrae mortis** Follows LXX. Whether the Hebrew phrase alludes explicitly to death is debated. It may be pointed to mean 'in a totally dark valley'. Christian exegetes sometimes interpreted the 'shadow of death' to allude to the semblance of death that occurred when one was buried with Christ in baptism.

Virga ... baculus 'rod ... staff'. In Hebrew the distinction is between a rod or club to protect and a staff to support.

22.5 **Parasti** The image of the Lord changes from that of a shepherd to that of a host at a banquet. In Christian exegesis, the banquet is sometimes interpreted as eschatological.

Inpinguasti in oleo caput meum 'You have annointed (literally, You have fattened) with oil my head'. It was a respectful gesture of welcome for a host to anoint a guest's head with oil. *In* reflects Hebrew itrumental b$^\theta$. *inpinguasti* (= LXX ἐλίπας) reflects the Hebrew root d-š-n, 'to be fat', which in the piel, a sometimes causative verbal pattern, means 'to cause to be fat, fatten, enrich, or annoint'. To Augustine, the oil is spiritual joy.

inebrians Not 'overflowing' but more exactly 'inebriating, exhilarating'. In Christian Latin, inebriation may refer to reception of the Holy Spirit. Also, the cup is sometimes taken as a reference to the Eucharist.

22.6 **omnibus diebus vitae meae** The ablative, instead of the accusative, expresses extent of time.

22.7 **Et ut inhabitem** The *ut* clause is substantival and based on LXX's articular infinitive construction (τὸ κατοικεῖν με) which reproduces a Hebrew infinitive construct 'my dwelling, living'. 'And (this) that I dwell in the house of the Lord, (may it be) for length of days.' A simpler, and so probably unoriginal, variant is *et inhabitabo*.

in longitudinem dierum Literally, 'for length of days'. The translation follows closely LXX which in turn is modelled on the Hebrew. The exact sense is 'for the course of a long life', not 'forever'.

Psalm 23

Like Psalm 14, a liturgical Psalm perhaps recited by pilgrims on their way to Jerusalem.

23.1 **Prima sabbati** '(To be recited) on the first day of the week'. *sabbati* = genitive. This undateable liturgical direction perhaps arose out of the Psalm's use in the synagogue. It may also be connected with the traditional notion that creation, part of the Psalm's theme, began on the first day of the week. It occurs in some Greek manuscripts but not in MT. To Augustine the Psalm relates to Christ's resurrection. Christian tradition also employed the Psalm on the feast of the Ascension.

Domini Emphatic by its position, the genitive stresses complete ownership.

et plenitudo eius 'and its fullness', i.e. 'and all that fills it, its abundance'. The Latin follows the Greek which literally reproduces the Hebrew **m^e lô 'āh**, 'its fullness'. The abstract noun is used for the concrete.

universi In later Latin *universus, cunctus*, and *totus* (the last especially in popular language) replace *omnis*.

23.2 **Quia ipse** ... Justifies the previous statement.

super maria ... super flumina The Hebrew reference is cosmogonic and refers to the establishment of kingship over the forces of chaos.

fundavit eum ... praeparavit eum Augustine's text read *eam* and he interprets the pronoun to refer to the Church.

23.3 **Quis ascendit** To account for the abrupt transition some scholars divide the Psalm into three distinct parts: hymn to the creator (1-2), Tôrāh liturgy specifying qualifications for admission to the sanctuary (3-6), and procession liturgy (7-10).

montem Domini Zion.

23.4 **manibus ... corde** Deed and thought are juxtaposed to render the description comprehensive.

qui non accepit in vano animam suam As it stands, the Latin might be rendered 'who has not admitted (= handed over) his soul into that which is vanity (= evil)'. Cf. Augustine's interpretation: *qui non in rebus non permanentibus deputavit animam suam*. The ablative is either pregnant (anticipating the result) or static used for a directional accusative as is typical in both later Greek and Latin. The word translated *accipere* might better have been translated *elevavit*. 'To lift up one's soul to' in Hebrew = 'long for'. The Hebrew word underlying *vanum* is often an oblique way of referring to an idol as 'something useless'; thus: 'who has not worshipped an idol'.

in dolo Expresses manner = *dolose*.

23.5 **misericordiam** 'mercy', after LXX ἐλεημόσυνη, but originally the Hebrew word = 'righteousness' and by extension 'vindication'.

23.6 **Haec est generatio** = Greek γενεά, a too literal translation of the Hebrew word which may mean 'generation' in some contexts but here perhaps = 'sort of person'. 'This is a type of men (or group) whose characteristic it is ...'. Note Augustine's overinterpretation: *sic enim nascuntur qui quaerunt eum.*

23.7 **Adtollite ... vestras** Transition to the third component of the Psalm, a processional liturgy. As the ark of the covenant is brought up to Zion, *principes* (= leaders, i.e. priests and Levites) are first addressed, then the gates themselves. The imperatives *adtollite* and *elevamini* are not to be taken literally. They are hyperbolic and suggest that the gates of human dimensions must be heightened to receive *rex gloriae.*

portae aeternales Hebrew 'gates of eternity' may refer to 'heavenly gates' or simply 'long-lasting gates'. The Latin preserves the ambiguity since *aeternus* may be used in an attenuated sense of structures that are 'durable, lasting'. Augustine's interpretation is *aditus aeternae vitae.*

rex gloriae 'king of glory', i.e. 'glorious king'.

23.8 **iste** Generally loses any since of reproach.

Dominus virtutum In ecclesiastical writers *virtus* undergoes changes of meaning: 'power, manifestation of power', hence 'miracle'; also 'force, act of force, army'. From verse 8 the military meaning is appropriate here, 'Lord of hosts'. So also Greek δύναμις. **Yhwh ṣᵉbā'ôt** is an obscure phrase that may have meant different things in different periods: e.g. *Deus omnipotens*, ṣᵉbā'ôt being an intensive plural, i.e. a plural that intensifies the idea of the singular.

ipse Corresponds to the Hebrew third person pronoun which is used in place of a verbal copula: 'Yahweh of hosts He (= is) the king of glory.' The Latin idiomatically adds *est.*

Psalm 25

Originally, an individual lament containing an appeal of an innocent person falsely accused.

25.1 **Iudica** The word's semantic range is similar to that of its Hebrew counterpart: 'judge, deliver, defend, vindicate'.

quoniam Represents the Hebrew particle ki which here may be emphatic (= 'indeed', i.e. I swear) rather than logical (= 'because of the fact that').

in innocentia mea ingressus sum For the Hebraic way of describing one's mode of conduct, see on *abiit*, 1.1.

innocentia The Latin word suggests exemplary 'freedom from guilt' or an absolute 'integrity'. The Hebrew word portrays the righteous man's proper attitude relative to the covenant ordinances.

et in Domino sperans non infirmabor *non infirmabor* may be translated 'I shall not lose confidence'. The Hebrew literally is: 'and in Yahweh I trusted (perfect) so that I will not waver (imperfect)'. The imperfect perhaps represents a logical consequence of the action of trusting. Alternatively it may be circumstantial = 'without wavering'.

25.2 **Proba ... ure** The imagery derives from metallurgy.

renes meos et cor meum i.e. 'my whole being'. The kidneys and heart are the two most important internal organs in the OT. The kidneys are the seat of emotions something like the conscience. Cf. 15.7: *in super et usque ad noctem increpuerunt me renes mei*. lēḇ (= cor) is the seat of both emotional and intellectual activities.

25.3 **misericordia tua ante oculos meos est** *misericordia* = ḥeseḏ, loyalty to the covenant. The pronominal suffix represented by *tua* may be objective in Hebrew ('the loyalty towards You'). The sentence would then be a statement of one's adherence to the covenant. In Latin, however the natural interpretation would be 'Your compassion is before my eyes' = is manifested.

conplacui in 'I have taken pleasure in', after LXX's paraphrase. Hebrew has 'I have walked in' = 'I have modelled my conduct on'.

veritate tua To Augustine, 'Your (God's) truth', but originally not 'truth' but 'sincerity, faithfulness' (to promises). *tua* may again be objective, 'faithfulness to You' and thus parallel to *tua* modifying *misericordia* above. See on *veritates* 11.2.

25.4 **vanitatis** Abstract for concrete. Translates LXX's abstract ματαιότητος, Hebrew 'worthless men'. The Hebrew word for vanity may also refer sometimes to an idol, an empty useless thing.

introibo Reproduces LXX's mistranslation of the Hebrew verb which here means not 'enter, go in', but simply 'go, consort with'. The shift to the future tense (cf. preceding *sedi*) formally and too simply reproduces the Hebrew imperfect. Cf. NIV's more accurate translation, 'I do not sit with ... nor do I consort with ...'.

iniqua gerentibus The Hebrew more exactly = 'dissemblers, the duplicitous'.

25.5 **Odivi** In V *odi* is conjugated as though from *odire*.

ecclesiam 'assembly'.

malignantium 'of evildoers'. The post-classical verb (*maligno* or *malignor*) is derived from the adjective.

cum impiis Cf. 1.1 where rᵉšăʿîm is also translated *impiorum*. The term refers to God's enemies whether Jew or Gentile.

25.6   **inter innocentes** 'among the innocent' expressing manner indirectly through location. The Hebrew is directly modal: 'in innocency'.

25.7   **vocem** 'sound'.

25.9   **animam meam** Virtually = to *vitam meam* below.

   viris sanguinum A Hebraism = 'murderers, bloodthirsty men'.

25.10   **muneribus** 'with bribes'. The text may equally refer to those who give bribes or those who accept them.

25.11   **Ego autem** Emphatic and contrastive with the evildoers.

25.12   **stetit** The Hebrew perfect may describe the past activity of the psalmist or be a so-called perfect of certainty relating to the future. 'shall (surely) stand'.

   in directo 'on level (ground)'. May be taken literally to refer to the level temple court and figuratively in a moral sense.

   ecclesiis Probably 'assemblies' of worshippers, but to Augustine, 'the churches'. The Hebrew plural may also be emphatic and hence = 'the great assembly' of the Godfearing in Israel who come together to worship in the temple.

Psalm 31

Originally a Psalm of thanksgiving, but in Christian tradition the second Penitential Psalm

31.1   **Huic David** *Huic*, like *ipsi* elsewhere, marks the case of David as dative and reflects the Greek definite article: (τῷ Δαυείδ).

   intellectus Probably genitive corresponding to Greek συνέσεως, which may express purpose. Cf. the alternative translation εἰς σύνεσιν ('for understanding'). Thus '(a Psalm) of David for instruction'. A Latin reader might take it as a genitive of description = *dans intellectum*. MT has maskîl which is obscure and translated variously ('didactic poem, artistically devised song').

   Iniquitates The Hebrew pešaʿ means more precisely rebellion against God's authority.

tecta sunt The Latin would naturally mean 'have been covered, concealed'. Cf. Augustine's interpretation's *in oblivionem ducta sunt*. The Hebrew notion is 'to cover' so as to offend the eye no longer.

31.1-2 **peccata ... peccatum** Hebrew ḥᵃṭṭāʾāh, 'failure, error' and ʿāwōn, 'perversion' or 'going astray' from God's will. The Hebrew words for sin are stylistical variants within parallel sentences. Their meanings are not sharply distinguished.

31.2 **spiritu** Hebrew rûaḥ is semantically fluid and = *voluntas*, but not quite = 'free will'. It is an impulsive force within a man that may be positive or negative.

31.3 **Quoniam** Probably causal after LXX's ὅτι.

Tacui 'I made no utterance', i.e. failed to acknowledge openly my guilt.

Ossa The last part of the body left after corruption and so figuratively portraying a truly desperate situation.

dum clamarem The *dum* clause denotes the cause of the main action – *inveterare*: His exhaustion comes from his continuous crying out. Cf. LXX ἀπὸ τοῦ κράζειν με ... and Seneca, *dum docent discunt* 'they learn from teaching'. The verb may be subjunctive or indicative with *dum* causal.

tota die The ablative is used to express duration of time.

31.4 **conversus sum in aerumna mea** 'I turned (writhed?) in my misery'. The Hebrew text is disputed and so translations vary: e.g. NIV: 'My strength was sapped as in the heat of summer.'

Spina To Christian exegetes, a figure for sin.

31.6 **Pro hac** = *propter hoc*. The use of the feminine for the neuter is a Hebraism. A Latin reader would more naturally take *hac* as referring to *impietatem;* Augustine does so.

Orabit The Hebrew imperfect here is volitional and thus more exactly = *oret*.

Sanctus Hebrew ḥāsîd, 'godly', one who follows the ordinances of the covenant.

in tempore oportuno 'in due season'. The Hebrew text is probably corrupt and is sometimes corrected to 'in a time of distress'.

Verumtamen In classical Latin 'nevertheless' but here an affirmative particle = 'surely'. The difficulty arises from an inadequate literal translation of Hebrew raq which may function as both a limiting and asseverative conjunction. Also the Hebrew text may be corrupt.

in diluvio aquarum multarum The Hebrew refers to a sudden flash flood. Augustine interprets the phrase eschatologically and figuratively = multitude of false doctrines. *Eum* in his interpretation refers to God, not to *sanctus*. The original figure perhaps referred simply to overwhelming troubles.

31.8   **Intellectum tibi ...** God is probably the speaker.

firmabo ... oculos meos 'I shall fix my eyes'; *oculos firmare* usually = 'to put on a set look'.

31.9   **In camo et freno** 'with bit and bridle'. After the Hebrew, *in* is instrumental.

constringe The 'binding' imperative shifts the imagery abruptly after 'don't become like a horse or mule' and reflects underlying textual difficulties. The sense is fairly clear. Don't be like an irrational animal that will not come to someone unless it is controlled by the bit and bridle.

Qui The antecedent is *eorum*.

31.10   **flagella** Contrasted with the following *misericordia*.

31.11   **iusti ... recti corde** Virtually synonymous.

Psalm 37

The third so-called Penitential Psalm. Originally an individual lament perhaps of one afflicted by disease.

37.1   **in rememorationem** 'for remembrance', = LXX's εἰς ἀνάμνησιν, a possible rendering of the Hebrew. The obscure phrase is sometimes interpreted as reflecting cultic practice, specifically the memorial offering of Leviticus 2.2. It may also mean no more than 'to cause (God) to remember (the psalmist's sufferings)'.

de sabbato Again following LXX but not in MT. A liturgical insertion which seems to specify a day of the week for the Psalm. *de* reproduces LXX's περί, hardly the normal prepostion to specify time of recital, but the Greek may be Hebraizing: περί = semantically fluid l^θ, '(belonging) to the Sabbath'. In later Latin, *de* would have been interpreted genitivally.

37.2   **ne ... arguas ... neque corripias** In classical Latin prose the perfect subjunctive is normal in such prohibitions. Cf. 22 below.

37.3   **sagittae** Here the bearers of disease as in Canaanite and Greek tradition.

confirmasti super me manum tuam 'You have made strong Your hand upon me', i.e. You have made me feel the force of Your hand.

37.4   **carni** 'flesh' has many connotations in Hebrew. Here weakness in front of God may be stressed.

a facie irae tuae ... a facie peccatorum meorum Follows LXX's too literal translation of a Hebrew semipreposition (preposition with noun, usually part on body). The noun part generally loses its specific reference: *a facie* = *a*, which may be translated here 'because of'. Causal *a*, found in Lucretius and Livy, becomes especially common in ecclesiastical Latin.

Pax Reproduces Greek εἰρήνη which in turn is based on Hebrew šālôm (wholeness, health, prosperity, peace). A better translation of the Hebrew here would have been 'health'.

Ossibus Flesh and bones is a Hebraic way of referring to one's entire body or being.

37.5   **supergressae sunt caput meum** i.e. like a powerful flood.

37.6   **cicatrices** 'wounds', sometimes taken perhaps too specifically as a reference to leprosy.

Insipientiae In Hebrew not simply 'foolishness', but 'folly' with religious connotations. See on *insipiens*, 13.1.

37.7   **usque ad finem** 'utterly, altogether'.

37.8   **lumbi** The place of procreation and so symbolic of strength and vitality.

Inlusionibus 'with illusions, mockeries'. The Hebrew would seem to = *inflammatione*. The sentence may mean 'My loins have become an object of mockery'.

37.10   **Domine ante te omne desiderium meum** 'Lord, before You (lies) all that I desire', specifically the wish to be healed.

37.11   **virtus mea** 'my strength, vigour'.

lumen oculorum Often used of vitality.

et ipsum 'it (the light) too'.

37.12   **Amici mei et proximi mei adversus me adpropinquaverunt et steterunt et qui iuxta me erant de longe steterunt** The parallelism of the two sentences precludes the easy interpretation of *adversum* as hostile 'against': 'My friends and my relatives have approached opposite me and stood still. My neighbours (those who were near me) have stood far off.' Cf. Jer. *cari mei et amici mei*

quasi contra lepram meam steterunt et vicini mei longe steterunt.
The Hebrew text is somewhat muddled but may mean 'My companions and those that love me stood back from my plague and my neighbours stood at a distance.'

de longe 'far off'.

Faciebant Better, *fecerunt*. The imperfect too literally renders the Hebrew progressive imperfect. Its time reference here is actually that of *adpropinquaverunt ... steterunt*; 'they have approached' (or simply 'they approach') and so 'they have done' (or 'do') violence.

37.13   **vanitates** 'falsehoods'.

Meditabantur Parallel to *locuti sunt*; hence 'they kept murmuring'.

37.14   **non audiebam** His passivity arises from a conviction that his troubles come ultimately from God as punishment.

37.15   **redargutiones** 'rebuttals', i.e. defence.

37.17   **Quia** Gives a second reason for his passivity.

dum commoventur pedes mei 'while my feet faltered', in Hebrew, a way of describing misfortune.

super me 'over (or against) me'.

magna locuti sunt = 'they boasted, exalted themselves'.

37.18   **ego in flagella paratus** Describes the speaker's dire predicament and not his voluntary subservience to disasters. *in* = 'for'.

37.19   **cogitabo** Seemingly too neutral to render adequately the more intense Greek and Hebrew verbs which = 'I shall be anxious about, be troubled by', but the word in later Latin may mean 'be indecisive, perplexed'.

37.21   **detrahebant** 'they slandered' with dative in place of classical *de me.*

37.22   **non** *non* for *ne* in a prohibition is rare in classical Latin.

37.23   **Intende** 'turn, direct Your efforts', after LXX's πρόσχες. The Hebrew has 'make haste' which perhaps sounded irreverent to the LXX translators.

Domine salutis meae See on *deus iustitiae meae*, 4.2

Psalm 38

Originally, an individual lament.

38.1   **Idithun** The obscure heading perhaps assigned the Psalm to the family of Jeduthun, one of David's chief musicians. In LXX the noun is marked as dative which case roughly corresponds to Hebrew l⁰. ('to, for, by'). Augustine etymologizes the name as 'one who overleaps them' who cling to the earth and are preoccupied by temporal things.

Canticum = LXX ᾠδή, Hebrew mızmôr, which elsewhere is rendered ψαλμός, *psalmus* without detectable difference.

38.2 **Dixi** A literal translation of the Hebrew, here better rendered 'I have decided, I am resolved.'

vias meas 'my ways' refers to mode of conduct, 'how I act'.

custodiam After LXX's φυλακήν, a dilution of the Hebrew metaphor: 'muzzle'.

cum Expresses the circumstances of the silence 'while, so long as'.

Adversum Probably not 'against' but simply 'opposite, in front of'. Cf. LXX ἐναντίον. To Augustine, *adversum* = *contra*, the normal sense of the word in his time.

38.3 **silui a bonis** Literally, 'I was silent from good things' = 'I said not even anything good'. The precise meaning of mıṭṭôḇ ('from good') is disputed ('to no avail, without effect'). The use of *a* with *silere* reflects Hebrew usage.

38.4 **Concaluit cor meum** 'my heart grew hot', in Hebrew, not a reference to anger but to uncontrollable anxiousness.

Exardescet The future renders the Hebrew imperfect, which here would have been better translated as a perfect.

38.5 **notum fac** Closely corresponds to the hiphil (causative) imperative of the verb 'to know' in the Hebrew.

quis est *quis* refers to *numerum*. Note indicative *est* rather than the subjunctive. As in Plautine Latin, the question is coordinated with the imperative, *notum fac*, rather than subordinated. The use of the indicative in indirect questions becomes common in later Latin.

quid desit mihi 'what is lacking to me', i.e. 'my deficiency, how frail I am'.

38.6 **mensurabiles** 'measurable, capable of being (easily) measured', i.e. short. The Hebrew is 'handbreadths', very small units of measure.

Substantia Here = 'life, existence', Hebrew, 'duration of life'. Cf. Augustine: 'before You, where Your eyes are, and not where the eyes of men are, I am as nothing'. His interpretation suggests a deeper meaning implicit in *substantia*, 'that which lies below, real being' in contrast to what is above, visible. The underlying Greek word ὑπόστασις varies widely in meaning in LXX. Cf. 38.8 below.

Verumtamen Here = *profecto*, 'surely'.

Universa According to the Greek, nominative plural neuter, 'all things are ...' but Augustine takes it as nominative feminine singular modifying *vanitas*.

38.7 **in imagine** = *ut imago*. More precisely it reflects the Hebrew *beth essentiae* or beth ('in') of identity, 'in essence, a mere shadow'.

Frustra 'to no end'.

conturbatur 'he troubles himself'.

Thesaurizat 'he lays up treasures'. From Greek θησαυρίζω. For similar Greek derivatives, cf. *prophetizare, scandalizare*.

38.8 **expectatio mea** 'object of my hope'.

nonne Dominus 'is it not the Lord?'

substantia mea Here, 'that which stands beneath, supports me; my means of support'.

38.9 **obprobrium insipienti dedisti me** 'You have made me an object of scorn to the fool'. *insipiens*, a collective singular translates Hebrew nāḇāl, the 'fool' who has shut his mind to God and His ordinances. *dare* = 'make, render' is found in colloquial Latin but becomes more common in ecclesiastical Latin possibly under Hebrew influence. The reading of MT is probably correct here, 'do not make me ...'.

38.10 **quoniam tu fecisti** 'since it was You who did this'; explains the psalmist's silence. His misfortune is an act of God and the result of his sinful state. How can he complain?

38.12 **A fortitudine manus tuae ego defeci in increpationibus** 'because of the strength of Your hand I have been consumed in punishments'. Causal *a* reflects Greek ἀπό, Hebrew min.

Araneam 'Spider' as in LXX against Hebrew 'moth'. The latter is a symbol of fleeting existence or destructiveness. The spider was thought to waste away its own substance in making its web.

38.13 **deprecationem** 'supplication'.

Ne sileas 'do not remain silent'.

Advena 'stranger, visitor from abroad'. gēr, in Hebrew, is a 'permanent resident, alien'.

Peregrinus 'sojourner, foreign settler'. In Hebrew a tôšāḇ, a temporary, landless, wage earner, resides less permanently than a gēr, but the two here are virtually synonymous. The petitioner, an alien in the Lord's land, like his forefathers entrusts himself to God.

38.14   **Remitte mihi** LXX ἄνες μοι. An appropriate and idiomatic translation of the Hebrew 'look away from me' which here means 'don't regard me for judgement'. Cf. Jer. *parce mihi.*

Refrigerer 'be restored'. In pagan literature *refrigerare* = 'to cool', but in Christian, it and *refrigerium* come to refer to refreshment in the sense of eternal life or blessedness.

Abeam 'go away', in the sense 'die'.

et amplius non ero The use of *ero*, instead of subjunctive *sim* coordinated with abeam after *priusquam,* follows LXX's parataxis.

Psalm 41

Originally, an individual lament perhaps of one separated from temple and home. In Roman Catholic liturgy the Psalm was traditionally connected with the rite of baptism for adults.

41.1   **In intellectum** Translates LXX's εἰς σύνεσιν. See on 31.1, *intellectus.*

filiis Core '(belonging) to the sons of (i.e. 'clan of') Korah'. The phrase perhaps originally classified this Psalm and other Psalms as having come from the repertoire of this guild of temple singers. Korah with the Levites rose up against the priestly family of Aaron over the issue of cultic privileges (Numbers 16). *Core* follows LXX's transliteration Κορε. To Augustine, *Core = Caluaria* (the place of Christ's crucifixion) = Christ. The Psalm then becomes the words of the Christian faithful or the Catechumens hurrying to the grace of the waters of Baptism.

41.2   **cervus** Properly 'stag' but here 'deer'. Exactly = the masculine Hebrew word which here however is construed exceptionally as feminine (hind) because it occurs with a feminine verb form. The Greek word, itself epicene (masculine or feminine), is preceded by the feminine article.

desiderat ... ad Reproduces the Greek ἐπιποθεῖ ... ἐπί ('longs for') which in turn imitates Hebrew syntax. *Desiderare* would normally take the accusative without preposition.

fontes aquarum A translation of πηγὰς τῶν ὑδάτων.

41.3   **Sitivit ... ad Deum** Again the preposition occurs through Hebrew influence. Latin would normally use the simple accusative.

Deum fortem = θεὸν τὸν ἰσχυρὸν the reading of some LXX manuscripts. ἰσχυρόν is either a gloss of Hebrew 'ēl or a translation as though it were adjectival rather than a Divine name = θεός.

vivum In Hebrew suggests a parallel with *fontes aquarum* since flowing waters are often called 'living'.

parebo ante faciem Dei A way of alluding to a temple visit.

41.4 **Fuerunt ... nocte** A vivid way of describing profound, continual mourning whether accompanied by fasting or not.

41.5 **Haec** Should refer to what follows: *quoniam transibo*.

recordatus sum et effudi Reproduces LXX's aorists which inadequately render the Hebrew cohortative 'let me recall ... let me pour out'. The cohortatives express deliberate effort.

effudi in me animam meam Follows LXX which in turn reproduces Hebrew. 'I have poured out my soul (which is) in (or upon) me', an idiom used to express great sorrow. The **nepeš** (= anima) is the central organ of suffering. In Vergil, *effundere animam* = 'die', but the problem here lies in 'in me'. From the Hebrew, it appears better to take it with *animam* rather than *effudi*.

transibo The Hebrew imperfects are rendered as futures in LXX and so in V. Since they represent actions recollected, they should have been translated as imperfects of customary action. Thus, the Hebrew is properly = 'how I used to go ...'.

in loco Ultimately reflects Hebrew b^e ('in' or 'into') but also in later Latin the distinction between *in* with the ablative and *in* with the accusative was blurred.

usque ad *usque* normally emphasizes the idea of direction.

in voce Modifies *transibo* and expresses manner.

exultationis et confessionis The adnominal genitives modify voce. *confessio* = 'praise'.

sonus epulantis 'the (proper) sound of one [collective singular] celebrating the feast'. *Sonus* is either genitive in apposition to *exultationis et confessionis* or an unattached nominative.

41.6 **salutare vultus mei** Literally, 'saving help of my face' = 'salvation of my person, my salvation'. In Hebrew the final suffixed pronoun modifies the whole construct chain and 'face' sometimes = 'self, person'.

41.7 **Ad me ipsum** = LXX's πρὸς ἐμαυτόν. Which here would have been better translated *in me ipso*.

de terra ... a monte The geography may specify the location of the speaker or have some deeper significance no longer completely recoverable. The locations are in northern Israel where the Jordan River has its sources and so perhaps there is a continuation of the water imagery of verse 2 above and following. The plural *Hermoniim* 'Hermons' may refer to the entire Hermon mountain range. Syntactically it may be correlative to *tui* and thus genitive rather than dependent on *de*. *Monte modico* follows the Greek translation of the Hebrew proper name Mizar ('little mountain'). The geographical enumeration moves from the general (*terra Jordanis*) to the specific (*Hermoniim*) to the more specific (*monte modico*).

41.8 **Abyssus ... invocat** In Hebrew, a way of saying trouble follows upon trouble. Cf. also Augustine who relates it to God's threat of further punishment for men even after all that they have suffered.

in voce A Hebraism reproduced by the Greek = 'at the sound of'.

excelsa tua Literally, 'your heights', possibly a mistranslation of LXX's οἱ μετεωρισμοί σου, 'your surges (at sea)'.

41.9 **In die mandavit Dominus misericordiam suam et nocte canticum eius** The underlying Hebrew is difficult but may mean 'By day the Lord has commanded loyalty to His covenant and by night His song'. In Christian Latin *misericordia* generally = 'mercy' and *mandavit* sometimes = *emittere*. Thus the possible translation, 'by day God has sent out His mercy and by night (there shall be) song to Him' (objective genitive, *eius* = reflexive here). Cf. the revised Psalter translation approved by Pius XII (1945): *per diem largiatur Dominus gratiam suam et nocte canam ei*. The word *misericordia* is obviously the core of the problem.

apud me Should be taken, at least according to LXX and MT, with *canticum eius*.

oratio In apposition to *canticum*.

Deo vitae meae The Hebrew may be rendered 'to the God of my life', i.e. 'to the God who gives me life' or 'my living God', the pronoun modifying the whole construct chain.

41.10 **susceptor** Follows LXX's translation which avoids the vivid Hebrew 'rock'.

41.11 **Dum ... ossa mea** i.e. while I was completely helpless; but a notion of causality may also be present: they reproached me for my helplessness.

Psalm 42

Treated as a separate Psalm in LXX and MT, this Psalm is generally considered to form a liturgical unit with the preceding Psalm.

42.1 **Iudica** 'judge' but also possibly 'vindicate'.

discerne 'judge, settle', but the Latin may also be translated 'separate' as Augustine takes it.

de Literally, 'from', i.e. '(so as to deliver) from'.

gente non sancta Originally, not necessarily gentiles but possibly Jews disloyal to the covenant.

homine Translates Hebrew ʾîš , probably a collective singular.

42.2 **Deus fortitudo mea** In Hebrew, a construct chain, 'the God of my stronghold', i.e. 'the God in whom I take refuge'.

42.3 **lucem ... veritatem** Here virtually personified messengers of God. To Augustine they are one and the same being, Christ. In Hebrew ʾᵉmet would have referred to 'fidelity' (to the covenant), not 'truth'.

Deduxerunt Not 'have led down' but 'have guided', *de* merely reinforcing the sense of *duco*. The tense follows LXX's aorist but MT has cohortative imperfect, 'let them guide'.

tabernacula tua The plural in Hebrew may serve to intensify a noun and does not necessarily indicate number. Here the sanctity of the temple is emphasized.

42.4 **iuventutem meam** Based on LXX's misinterpretation τὴν νεότητά μου which probably was occasioned by the Hebrew's redundancy: 'God the gladness of my joy'. Cf. Jer. *Deum laetitiae et exultionis meae.*

42.5 **salutare vultus mei** = *meum salutare*, 'my salvation'. On *vultus*, cf. 41.6.

Psalm 50

Of the seven so-called Penitential Psalms, Ps. 50 is usually regarded as the most important. Before modern reforms to the Roman Breviary, it was recited seven times a day. Even its number 50, to some commentators, had a hidden significance.

50.2 **cum ... Bethsabee** Probably a secondary accretion. Cf 3.1. David committed adultery with Bethsheba and then arranged her husband Uriah's death. The prophet Nathan publicly rebuked him for his sin. Cf. 2 Samuel 11-12.

intravit Reflects Hebrew bô', 'go, enter', which here refers to sexual intercourse.

Bethsabee Note in the spelling the tendency to substitute *s* for *sh*, a difficult sound for Latin speakers.

50.3 **secundum** 'in accordance with, as befits'.

multitudinem miserationum The abstract substantive with genitive, essentially = adjective with noun, reflects Hebrew influence.

miserationum tuarum Christian exegetes attached significance to the plural (e.g. David's sin was actually one but came under several forms and so required more than one act of grace to be cleansed). In fact, the Hebrew word occurs only in the plural in the sense 'mercy'.

iniquitatem The Hebrew is more specific: **peša'**, the fundamental sin of rebellion against God.

50.4 **Amplius** Represents the Hebrew hiphil imperative of the verb rābāh ('be great') which here is virtually adverbial = 'exceedingly'. It intensifies the Hebrew verb corresponding to *lava*.

lava The Greek and Hebrew words for 'wash' are used of clothes ('launder', Hebrew 'tread upon') but *lava*, which may be used of a *latrina*, is no less vivid.

ab iniquitate mea The Hebrew is 'āwōn, an offence purposely committed.

a peccato meo Hebrew ḥaṭṭā'h, like Greek ἁμαρτία, is related to a verb meaning 'miss the mark'. The Hebrew has three different words for sin, virtual synonyms used to stress the comprehensiveness of the speaker's guilt.

50.5 **cognosco** 'I acknowledge'.

contra Not simply = *coram*, but with its proper notion of hostility.

50.6 **ut iustificeris** The purpose clause probably should not be linked to what immediately precedes ('I have sinned ... so that You may be justified'). Rather there may be an ellipsis: '(I am confessing) so that ...'; or the clause is to be construed loosely with the opening imperatives: 'take pity on me, etc ... in order that ...'. It would thus parallel the *secundum* phrases.

in sermonibus tuis Literally, 'in Your words', i.e. 'in the judgement which You pronounce'.

vincas Follows LXX's νικήσῃς which imports an Aramaic sense into the Hebrew root. Here it perhaps = 'You may be pure, blameless'.

cum iudicaris Probably based on a misinterpretation of LXX's ἐν τῷ κρίνεσθαι σε. The infinitive is middle, not passive: 'When You have a legal dispute (or adjudge)' not 'when You are judged'. In a Christological interpretation the verb was taken passively as alluding to Christ's trial before Pilate, who pronounced Him without guilt.

50.7 Ecce enim in iniquitatibus conceptus sum In Christian tradition, the verse is taken to refer to Original Sin. The Hebrew expression perhaps emphasized that the psalmist has been a lifelong sinner.

in peccatis The phrase, to Augustine, modifies *concepit*. Since all humans have sinned through Adam, only the infant not born of the work of Adam, Christ, is free from sin.

50.8 incerta et occulta sapientiae tuae manifestasti mihi 'The unascertained and hidden elements of Your wisdom You have made known to me.' In later Christian exegesis *sapientiae* is taken as = Christ and the 'hidden things' as the Incarnation, Passion, and Resurrection. From the Hebrew perspective, perhaps God's love of 'truth' (= loyalty or sincerity) and intimate sharing of hidden things with David are being cited as reasons for His forgiveness now.

50.9 Asparges ... lavabis The future reflects the Hebrew imperfect of injunction which here express a positive request.

hysopo A plant used in ceremonies of atonement and purification to sprinkle blood and water on people and things.

super nivem dealbabor 'I shall be whitened beyond snow', a Hebraism: 'I shall be made whiter than snow'.

50.11 Averte faciem Usually a sign of divine displeasure, but here the action expresses forgiveness.

50.12 crea Like its Hebrew counterpart, a word characteristic of God's activity.

spiritum In Hebrew practically = 'disposition'.

50.13 spiritum sanctum To Christians, the Holy Spirit, but originally probably a way of describing the efficacious *praesentia Dei*.

50.14 spiritu principali 'with noble spirit'; the same *spiritus* as in 12, above.

50.15   **vias tuas** 'the paths to You'.

50.16   **de sanguinibus** 'from bloodguilt', following the Greek's imitation of the Hebrew plural of composition ('pools, stains of blood').

  exultabit ... iustitiam tuam *exultare* in classical Latin is generally intransitive.

50.17   **labia mea aperies** The future is imperatival. Cf. Exodus 7.15. *Vade ad eum ... et stabis,* 'go to him and stand'.

50.18   **Quoniam** Hebrew kî is probably emphatic ('indeed') here rather than causal.

50.19   **Sacrificium Deo spiritus contribulatus** 'A sacrifice to God is a much afflicted (i.e. chastened) spirit'.

50.20   **Benigne fac ... Sion** 'Deal favourably with Zion'.

50.21   **acceptabis** 'You will take with pleasure', a common meaning in ecclesiastical writers. From *acceptare*, the intensive of *accipere*.

  sacrificium iustitiae Literally, 'a sacrifice of righteousness', i.e. 'a just, proper sacrifice', duly prescribed and offered in the right spirit.

  oblationes et holocausta 'offerings and whole-burnt-offerings'. (Hebre ʿôlāh v' kālîl.) The original distinction between the two is not known. In fact, they may be virtually synonomous, the parataxis being simply a way of emphasizing that the whole offerings were burnt on the altar.

  inponent ... vitulos = *inponentur ... vituli*. In imitation of Hebrew, the third person plural with indefinite subject may also be used in place of a passive.

  vitulos A very costly form of sacrifice.

Psalm 109

The most commonly cited OT text in the NT, especially important for its supposed allusions to the Ascension and for its Messianic typology. The date and original setting of this Psalm are much disputed, like Psalm 21. Like Psalm 2, it may have had a place in the king's enthronement ceremony. The corrupt Hebrew text with its unusual poetic images poses many unsettled difficulties.

109.1 **Dixit Dominus** Renders LXX's εἶπεν ὁ κύριος. MT has nᵉʾ um yhwh, 'utterance (or oracle) of Yahweh', a formula found in prophetic revelations.

Domino meo LXX similarly repeats: τῷ κυρίῳ μου. MT has 'an utterance of Yahweh to my master (ʾᵃdōnî)', i.e. the king. The speaker in this case is presumably the court prophet.

a dextris meis A position of honour. The plural probably follows the Greek (ἐκ δεξιῶν μου).

Donec 'until'. The Hebrew equivalent, often rendered 'until' is less restrictive than English 'until' and sometimes = 'while'. This is a possible but more unusual sense for *donec*. Christians interpreted the passage as alluding to the temporal interval of Christ's defeat of death and the terrors of Hell and more vaguely to the time period between the Ascension and the second coming.

ponam Not 'place' but factitive: 'make, render' as commonly in V. Cf. Ps. 43.14: *posuisti nos obprobrium vicinis nostris.*

scabillum 'a low stool, footstool' a common Near Eastern metaphor for subservience or subjugation since a victorious king put his feet on the necks of the defeated enemies.

109.2 **Virgam virtutis tuae** 'the rod (or sceptre) of Your power', following LXX's too literal translation of the Hebrew construct chain which properly = 'Your powerful rod'. To some exegetes an allusion to the preaching of the Gospel.

dominare The shift to the imperative, after future *emittet*, is the stylistic figure heterosis (alteration) which transforms the second verb into a promise to be fulfilled.

109.3 **Tecum principium in die virtutis tuae** 'with you is dominion on the day of your power', i.e. 'you have dominion ...'. The Latin depends on LXX's way of pointing the Hebrew text. Cf. MT: 'your people (will be) willing ones (i.e. will volunteer) on your day of power'. Both Hebrew and Greek texts here are seemingly corrupt. Augustine takes *principium* as 'beginning, source' and so = God, but the meaning 'dominion' is found in earlier Latin, e.g. Suetonius, and is the interpretation of Tertullian.

in die virtutis tuae In Hebrew may also = 'on the day of your muster', a military allusion. For the military meaning of *virtus*, see 23.10 *Dominus virtutum.*

in splendoribus sanctorum The Latin might be translated 'in the splendours of saints'. The Hebrew, being a construct chain, may mean 'in majesties of holiness' i.e. 'in holy splendour'. The plural in Hebrew may intensify or emphasize and not merely indicate number.

ex utero ante luciferum genui te 'From the womb before the daystar I bore you'. Cf. MT 'from dawn's womb you will have the dew of your youth', i.e. a vigorous army will early and readily attend you like God's gift of 'dew'. To some Christian exegetes *ante luciferum* means God bore Christ before the morning star (or for that matter anything) was created.

109.4   Iuravit Dominus A second oracular introduction.

secundum ordinem Melchisedech 'after the order of', i.e. 'in the line of'. A possible reference to the poorly attested sacerdotal kingship in early Judaism. The priest-king Melchizedek, in contrast to Aaron, offered a nonbloody sacrifice of bread and wine, a point not lost on later Christian commentators who viewed the offering as a type of Eucharist and Melchizedek as a type of Christ.

109.5   a dextris tuis Here in the position of a willing helper and protector.

confregit Renders the Greek aorist which in turn renders the Hebrew perfect. The Hebrew perfect here, however, actually represents a completed future action, confidently envisioned, a usage common in prophetic contexts (*perfectum confidentiae*).

109.6   Iudicabit in 'he will give judgement among'. The construction is Hebraizing.

implebit cadavera 'He shall fill (places) with corpses'.

conquassabit capita in terra multorum 'He shall crush the heads in the land of many'. The Hebrew has 'he shall strike the head over a large land' (= the wide earth?). LXX takes 'head' as a collective singular (and pluralizes to κεφαλάς, literally, 'heads' or = possibly to 'leaders'). Also LXX reads rabîm for rabbâh (wide, large); hence *multorum*.

109.7   De torrente in via bibet 'From a rushing stream on the way he will drink'. Problematic, but to some scholars a reference to part of the royal ritual during which the king drinks the power-giving waters of a brook (Giʿhon?). Alternatively an expression of the king's effective perseverance in pursuit of his enemies: 'on the way (against them he will not stop but) he will drink from a rushing stream and therefore triumph'. To Augustine, he = Christ, who drinks from the brook that represents the flow of human mortality.

propterea i.e. because the stream is power-giving.

exaltabit caput 'he will lift up his head (in truimph)'.

Psalm 119

The first of the so-called Songs of Ascents or Gradual Psalms (119-133), 119 contains elements of individual lament and thanksgiving.

119.1   Canticum graduum *Graduum* may have referred to the 'steps' taken by pilgrims as they journeyed to Jerusalem. In the patristic writers the word was interpreted mystically (vertical ascent to the heavenly Jerusalem, progress or steps toward sanctity, raising the heart toward God in prayer). In this Psalm, a pilgrim who has sojourned in distant, savage lands appears to be giving thanks to God for his rescue and return. To Augustine the sojourner is a wanderer from the heavenly Jerusalem.

Ad Dominum Emphatic by position, 'to the Lord (alone)'.

119.2   animam meam Hebrew nepeš with pronominal suffix here = simply 'me'.

a labiis iniquis Literally, 'from evil lips' i.e. 'from liars', a common synechdoche (part for the whole).

119.3   Quid detur tibi et quid adponatur tibi ad linguam dolosam Rhetorical questions directed to the enemy of the psalmist. The subjunctives are deliberative. *Et quid adponatur tibi*, lit. 'and what may be added (done further) to you', may be translated by an emphatic 'and more'. *ad* = 'in proportion to', i.e. '(as a suitable punishment) for'. To Augustine, the Lord asks the question of the speaker to test him.

119.4   Sagittae potentis acutae A forceful answer to the previous questions. Since the tongues of one's enemies and their bitter words are often likened to swords and arrows, by the principle of retribution, their punishment appears in this form. For the imagery cf. Ps. 63. 3-6. To Augustine, *sagittae* are the words of God that rouse love in the hearts which they transfix. Christian writers tend to interpret *potentis* as a reference to God but the Hebrew gibbôr probably meant simply 'a mighty man, a warrior'.

cum carbonibus desolatoriis For coals as a punishment for slandering cf. Ps. 140.10, *cadent super eos carbones. desolatoriis* = Greek ἐρημικοῖς = 'of the desert' or possibly = 'causing desolation'. The Hebrew refers specifically to the broom plant whose coals are proverbially long-lasting. Again, Augustine interprets positively: the coals desolate the place of carnal thought and secular affections to prepare it as a place of perpetual bliss for Christ.

119.5   **incolatus** 'sojourn'. In Christian Latin the word comes to refer to man's temporary sojourn on Earth.

prolongatus est Following the Greek translators who vocalized the consonantal Hebrew text mŭššak, = 'drawn out', while MT has Mešek nomads who lived far away by the Black Sea. 'Woe is me that I sojourn in Meshech'. The name in MT is used figuratively for hostile barbarians.

Cedar Second son of Ishmael, but the name here denotes a nomadic Arab tribe and is used generically like Mešek, i.e. remote barbarians. To Augustine, *Cedar* = *tenebrae* and represents the descendants of Ishmael (the old covenant, the earthly Jerusalem) against Isaac (the new covenant, the heavenly Jerusalem).

119.6   **multum** The corresponding Hebrew adverb of quantity may = 'much' or 'too long'.

incola 'foreigner'.

anima mea In the Hebrew, again a periphrasis for 'I'.

119.7   **gratis** In classical Latin, 'without recompense', but here 'without cause, unjustly', as in Ps. 118.161: *principes persecuti sunt me gratis.*

Psalm 121

Perhaps originally a pilgrimage song but the focus on Zion may be seen as eschatological and thus prepares the way for later Christian exegesis. To Augustine, a Psalm of those who long to ascend to heaven to the eternal Jerusalam.

121.1   **huic David** *huic* has no proper force but serves merely to mark the case of the indeclinable *David*. Cf. LXX: τῷ Δαυείδ.

Laetatus sum The speaker is a pilgrim who either has visited or is visiting the holy city.

In domum Domini ibimus In Hebrew a formulaic way of announcing a pilgrimage.

121.2   **Stantes erant pedes nostri** 'our feet were standing'. In classical Latin normally only a present participle which has become an adjective (e.g. *sapiens*) is used with *esse*. The periphrastic usage is characteristic of later Latin. In Hebrew the tense is ambiguous: either 'our feet were standing' or 'our feet have taken up their position, stand', i.e. 'our feet are standing'.

atriis Translates Greek αὐλαῖς, properly 'open court' before a house, but in MT 'gates'. The LXX translators may have been influenced by Aramaic which has a word whose semantic range is 'court, gate', or αὐλαῖς is a corruption of πυλαῖς. In Christian Latin *atrium* comes to be used of the square before a church.

121.3 **ut civitas** *ut* reflects the Hebrew particle kî which in some contexts means 'as, like' but here is a particle of asseveration 'truly a city – a real city', the so-called *kaph veritatis*. To Augustine, *ut* suggests that 'city' is not to be taken materially but spiritually.

cuius participatio eius in id ipsum *eius* imitates the so-called resumptive pronoun of Hebrew and so is superfluous. Thus, literally, 'the compactness of which is close together' (*participatio = conjunctio, in id ipsum = in unum*). The clause may refer to the compact, highly defensible nature of the city itself. But *participatio*, like its LXX counterpart μετοχή normally means 'fellowship'. Thus the alternative, 'whose fellowship (i.e. that of the tribes or pilgrims in it) is close'. To Augustine, *in id ipsum* = 'in the Same', i.e. in Him who never changes, Christ.

121.4 **Illic** = *illuc*, but has its usual meaning in 5 below.

tribus tribus In Hebrew, the repetition singles out the elements of the whole and is distributive = 'every tribe'. Latin *omnes tribus* would be a close, but ambiguous equivalent since *omnis* need not have distributive force.

tribus Domini A rare substitute for *tribus Israel.*

testimonium Here not 'testimony' but 'ordinance'. Cf. Deuteronomy 6.20 *a testimoniis tuis non declinavi*. Thus, *testimonium Israhel* = '(the practice) ordained to Israel', the phrase being loosely appositional to *ascenderunt tribus*.

ad confitendum 'to give praise to'.

121.5 **sedes** 'thrones' referring by metonymy to the Davidic kings. To Augustine *sedes* = the righteous.

super domum David *super* follows LXX's incorrect translation of the Hebrew preposition l⁰ which here = 'belonging to'; hence a genitive would have been a better translation.

121.6 **Rogate quae ad pacem sunt Ierusalem** Literally, 'ask for what things are for the peace of Jerusalem', i.e. 'pray for the prosperity of Jerusalem'.

et abundantia diligentibus te *abundantia* is either accusative neuter plural after *rogate* 'and for abundance for those who love you', or nominative feminine singular with *sit* understood, 'and may there be abundance for those who love you'. The second interpretation is closer to the Greek which approximates the Hebrew.

121.7 **Fiat pax in virtute tua** The Hebrew appears to be 'may salvation be in your ramparts', an indication of the broader semantic range of the words underlying *pax* and *virtute*. Cf. the following parallel phraseology *et abundantia in turribus fiat.*

121.8 **loquebar pacem de te** In Hebrew the words uttered are direct speech, a form of greeting or wish for prosperity. 'Peace now be within you.'

121.9 **bona** = LXX ἀγαθά; literally, 'good things', i.e. prosperity (MT ṭôḇ).

Psalm 122

In Hebrew a Psalm of lament, perhaps both individual and communal.

122.1 **Ad te** Emphatic: 'to You (and no one else)'.
levavi oculos meos In an attitude of prayer.

122.2 **oculi servorum in manibus dominorum suorum** The exact nuance of the figure is uncertain. The slaves may look to their masters' hands for punishment or await some gestural command or possibly gift of food. The basic notion is complete subservience and dependency. In the OT a 'slave of Yahweh' is a common phrase for a pious person.

122.4 **obprobrium ... superbis** Supply either *sumus* 'we are an object of reproach', or *sit*, invoking a curse upon the *abundantes* and *superbi.*
abundantibus 'to those who are prospering' = Greek τοῖς εὐθηνοῦσιν. Hebrew 'those who are at ease, free from trouble'.

Psalm 123

Originally a Psalm of communal thanksgiving.

123.1 **Nisi quia Dominus erat** 'If (it had) not (been) that the Lord was', i.e. 'If the Lord had not been'. Reproduces LXX's εἰ μὴ ὅτι which too literally renders Hebrew lû lê še, 'except that'.

in nobis Again follows LXX: ἐν ἡμῖν. The Hebrew preposition l⁰ is one of 'interest' here and the phrase is better translated *pro nobis*.

dicat nunc Israhel Originally, a conventional way of exhorting the people to prayer. *nunc* is not temporal but either emphatic or logical and consequential (=LXX δή = nā', the Hebrew particle of exhortation attached to the verb form).

123.2 **homines** Greek ἀνθρώπους, Hebrew 'ādām: '(mere) human beings', in contrast to Yahweh.

123.3 **forte** 'conceivably', a usual translation, is inappropriate since it would undercut the strong affirmation of faith. *Forte* serves as a filler to represent ἄν, the untranslatable Greek particle of contingency in a contrary to fact condition. Omit in translating. It does not, as many have thought, represent an inadequate translation of Greek ἄρα (= inferential 'then').

degluttissent From *deglutio,* 'swallow down', a post-classical word.

123.4 **forsitan** Here probably = *forte* above, but Augustine regards *forsitan* as an inadequate translation of ἄρα which he equates to Punic *iar* = Latin *putas*. His point is *forsitan* does not = 'perchance'.

123.5 **Torrentem pertransivit anima nostra** Subject and object are interchanged in LXX and so in V. Cf. MT: 'the stream would have passed over our soul'; 'our soul' = 'us' or 'our lives'. The shift to the indicative mode is only apparently grammatically inconsistent. The absence of an ἄν equivalent makes the unrealized action imaginatively realized and the certitude of what would have happened *sine Deo* is thus expressed.

forsitan ... intolerabilem Again subject and an object are inverted in LXX and so in V, but the Latin makes perfect sense.

intolerabilem 'unable to be endured, overwhelming'.

in captionem 'as prey'.

123.7 **passer** Greek στρουθός. The Hebrew is generic = *avis*.

contritus est *contero*: 'wear out, destroy'.

123.8 **qui fecit caelum et terram** A formula but also a final reminder of God's complete creative power contrasted with the frailty of *homines*.

Psalm 125

A song of thanksgiving perhaps originally associated with the exiles' return from the Babylonian captivity.

125.1   In convertendo Dominum The gerund with *in* unidiomatically reproduces the Greek articular infinitive with preposition. The infinitive's subject is accusative case: ἐν τῷ ἐπιστρέψαι κύριον is literally, 'in Lord restoring'. The Greek in turn reflects the Hebrew infinitive construction with bᵉ. In Jer. Jerome always replaces this construction with a more idiomatic *cum* clause: *Cum converteret Dominus.* The Biblical construction does occur in Augustine and so would not have been unintelligible.

    captivitatem Sion = *captivos.* Abstract for concrete. Cf. Dt. 30.3, *reducet Dominus Deus tuus captivitatem.* The phrase *convertere captivos* = 'to restore the captives' probably refers to the return from the Babylonian captivity but the Hebrew word may actually be = 'lot, fortunes' not 'captivity'. *Sion*, denoting Israel as a whole, is an unmarked genitive. Translate, 'when the Lord restored the captives of Zion'.

    sicut consolati Follows LXX, ὡς παρακεκλημένοι. The Hebrew is more vivid and better represented by Jer. *quasi somniantes,* 'like people dreaming'. There is little evidence for a root h-l-m ('be strong, be healed') to explain LXX's interpretation.

125.2   dicent = *dicetur.* Cf. Luke 12.20, *hac nocte animam tuam repetunt a te.* The active third person plural is used for the passive third singular impersonal.

    Magnificavit ... facere A Hebraism = *magnifice egit* or *magna fecit,* 'has done great things for'. Both *magnificare* and *multiplicare* are so used in place of adverbs to express repeated or intense action.

    cum eis = LXX μετ' αὐτῶν which too literally reproduces the Hebrew. The Hebrew preposition, in addition to 'with', may mean 'to'.

125.4   sicut torrens in austro Perhaps proverbial for a sudden change or transformation. The dry channels in the arid south after a winter rainfall could be suddenly transformed into raging torrents. *Austro* refers to the south-country and the Hebrew may better have been translated by the proper name Negev.

125.6   Euntes ibant Literally, 'going, they went', a Hebraism. The present participle represents the Hebrew infinitive absolute which here before its verb expresses continuance, an indefinitely prolonged state of action, 'they went on for a long time (regularly)'. In this sense the infinitive absolute usually, but not invariably, occurs after the verb.

Venientes ... venient Again a reflection of the Hebrew infinitive absolute here serving to emphasize the certainty of the action: 'they will surely come (back)'. In V, the infinitive absolute is also reproduced by the ablative of the cognate noun or the ablative of the gerund. Cf. Genesis 2.17 *morte morieris*, 'thou shalt surely die'.

manipulos 'sheaves' contrasted with the *semina* with which 'they' went out.

Psalm 126

Originally, a wisdom Psalm.

126.1   **Salomonis** Only Psalms 71 and 126 are attributed to Solomon. The ascription here probably originated in the unnecessary inference that 'house' in verse 1 refers to Solomon's temple. The ascription is absent from LXX and early Vulgate manuscripts.

aedificaverit domum The phrase may be taken in a literal, physical sense or figuratively: 'provide with numerous descendants'. Cf. Exodus 1.21, of the midwives who refused to obey Pharaoh's command to kill Hebrew males: *Et quia timuerant obsetrices Deum, aedificavit eis domos.*

civitatem The Hebrew word may be used concretely ('city') or may refer to the inhabitants. The concrete meaning of *civitas* is common in post-classical Latin but here Augustine interprets both *domum* and *civitas* as the community of the faithful.

126.2   **Vanum est ... somnum** The Latin is difficult because of mistranslations in LXX. Originally the juxtaposition of 'rise' and 'sit' probably reflected a pointless frenetic activity, like English 'up and down'. 'It is pointless for you to rise before dawn, to rise after you have rested, you who eat the bread of sorrow, when God has bestowed on His beloved sleep.' All human endeavour and activity is meaningless without God's help since He is the giver of everything.

manducatis In later Latin *edere*, whose conjugation presented confusing similarities to that of *sum*, is replaced by *comedere* and the more vulgar *manducare* (normally 'chew' in classical Latin); hence Italian *mangiare*, French *manger*.

panem doloris i.e. the bread earned by pain and toil.

Cum Translates LXX ὅταν which probably, according to its underlying Hebrew text, rendered Hebrew kî, a causal or emphatic particle (= 'surely'). MT has **ken** ('surely'?) The exact meaning of the clause in Hebrew has never been unanimously established (possibly, 'so much He gives to His beloved even in sleep'). The clause does not recommend inactivity but emphasizes God as the ultimate source of everything.

126.3 hereditas Domini filii The verb 'to be' is omitted: 'sons are a heritage from God'.

mercis fructus ventris 'A reward (is) the fruit of the womb'. *mercis = merces.*

126.4 ita filii excussorum MT has 'so are the sons of youth', i.e. 'so are the sons born in one's youth'. V follows LXX which points the consonants as a masculine plural participle 'of those shaken off, of the outcasts'. The translators may have had in mind the Babylonian exiles who on their return required large families to counter trouble at home. The arrow imagery of this passage may have influenced the Greek translation.

126.5 Beatus vir A formula reflecting wisdom influence. See on 1.1.

desiderium suum Follows LXX's τὴν ἐπιθυμίαν αὐτοῦ. possibly a mistranslation of the Hebrew *hapax legomenon* for 'quiver' in the Psalter.

ex ipsis 'from them', i.e. the sons.

in porta Among Jews, the forum to settle legal disputes. Augustine interprets the phrase as speaking 'in the open', then equates the gate to Christ.

Psalm 127

The Psalm contains wisdom elements and praises obedience to God.

127.1 Beati omnes qui A wisdom formula, which implicitly encourages emulation of the ideal expounded. See on 1.1, *beatus vir qui*.

qui ambulant in viis eius For this Hebrarism, see note on *abiit*, 1.1.

127.2   **quia** Corresponds to the Hebrew particle kî, which, though often causal, here may have emphatic force: 'surely'. Its peculiar position reflects the Hebrew word order.

manducabis For this verb in place of *edere*, see on 126.2 *manducatis*.

127.3   **vitis abundans** Referring to the wife's fertility and more generally her assistance in helping the house to prosper.

in lateribus domus tuae 'at (or perhaps 'amidst') the sides of your house'. The Hebrew word for 'side' also meant 'rearside', then 'recess at rear', and finally 'innermost part'. Cf. Jer.'s more correct *in penetrabilibus domus tuae*. The ideal is a fertile wife who keeps herself secluded.

novellae 'shoot', that will in due season bring forth fruit.

127.4   **benedicetur** Translates the Hebrew root **b-r-ḵ** which is used to denote a divine blessing in contrast to the more secular 'ašrê of Ps. 1.1.

127.5   **bona Hierusalem** 'the prosperity of Jerusalem'.

127.6   **pax super Israhel** Supply *sit*.

Psalm 128

Originally a Psalm of communal confidence.

128.1   **Saepe** Emphatic by position.

expugnaverunt The implicit subject is Israel's enemies. Hebrew often uses the third person plural indefinitely where both Latin and Greek would use the passive voice.

me The nation Israel.

a iuventute mea Perhaps a reference to the period when Israel was enslaved in Egypt.

dicat nunc Israhel A liturgical exhortation. See on 123.1.

128.2   **etenim** In the Latin, the sequence of thought is clumsy since it follows LXX's misrendering of Hebrew **gam** by καὶ γάρ. In addition to being causal, **gam** may also rarely be adversative. A better translation here, then, would have been *sed*.

non potuerunt mihi 'could not (prevail against) me'. The dative with *posse* reproduces the Greek which in turn imitates the Hebrew construction.

128.3   Supra dorsum meum fabricabantur peccatores Literally, 'upon my back, sinners were framing (i.e. devising) schemes', following LXX's interpretation of the Hebrew metaphor: 'The ploughers have ploughed upon my back'. The underlying Hebrew verb ḥāraš may mean 'engrave, plough', or 'devise', usually in a bad sense. The agricultural image may portray a severe whipping as a symbol of complete subjugation.

iniquitatem Follows LXX ἀνομίαν but the corresponding Hebrew word is obscure; it may continue the metaphor: 'their furrows'.

128.4   cervices The Hebrew refers to the rope or harness holding the ox that draws the plough.

128.6   faenum tectorum The grass on the roof of eastern houses sprouts quickly but without roots and protection from the sun quickly withers.

evellatur Grass on the roof would not normally be pulled up. The Hebrew may mean 'be drawn out' in the sense 'bud, sprout'.

128.7   De quo Instead of the simple ablative.

128.8   et non dixerunt ... vos Given the uselessness of this grass, there is no harvest blessing from those passing by.

Psalm 129

Originally, an individual lament. The sixth of the so-called Penitential Psalms.

129.1   De profundis Like its Hebrew counterpart, *profunda* may literally refer to the depths of the sea or be used figuratively to refer to the 'depths' of misfortune or sin. *de = ex*, a common usage in late Latin.

clamavi The underlying Hebrew perfect represents the situation as occurring simultaneously with the utterance and so may be rendered as a present.

129.2   Fiant aures tuae intendentes in Literally, 'let your ears become attentive to'. The participial construction, reflecting the Greek's literal translation of the Hebrew, repeats what has already been expressed by the simpler verb *exaudi*, 'hear attentively, heed'.

vocem deprecationis meae 'the sound of my prayer', a too literal renditon of the Hebrew construct chain = 'my suppliant voice'. For the construction, see note on *sacrificium iustitiae*, 4.6.

129.3   observabis 'mark, observe (critically)' or 'retain (so as to punish)'.

sustinebit 'will endure'. An important verse in the struggle against Novatianism which refused concessions to any who had compromised under the Decian persecution (AD 249-250).

129.4   Quia In the Latin, the transition is abruptly elliptical: (*sed non observabis*) *quia* ... . Behind *quia* lies the semantically fluid Hebrew adverb and conjunction kî which here may = 'surely' and not 'for'.

apud te Emphatic by position.

propitiatio 'atonement'. To Augustine the 'propitiation' is the sacrifice of Christ Himself. Cf. Romans 3.25: *ipse est propitiatio pro peccatis nostris*. The post-classical word is used in V only in relation to God.

propter legem tuam The underlying text is uncertain: hence, the varying translations. In some manuscripts, LXX has 'for the sake of Your name (or law)'; MT, probably correct, has 'that You may be feared'. In a Hebrew consonantal text, the two options would look much alike. To Augustine 'the law' is Christ's law of reflected love in Matthew 6.12 *dimitte nobis debita nostra, sicut et nos dimittimus debitoribus nostris.*

sustinui Here = 'wait for, hope in' a common meaning in Christian Latin although in some medieval commentators it is translated 'I endured You' in the sense 'I suffered Your chastisement'.

verbum Originally the oracle of salvation delivered by the temple priest, but to a Christian, Christ.

129.6   A custodia matutina usque ad noctem In the Latin, temporal phrases: 'from the morning watch even until night', but Hebrew **min** (= *a*) is used here to express comparison; Hence MT 'more than the watchmen watch for the morning'. The watchmen (possibly Levites in the temple) wait for the morning to perform sacrifices. The phrase is repeated in the Hebrew which probably confused the LXX translators.

Psalm 130

Originally an individual Psalm of confidence.

130.1 **non est exaltatum cor meum** Literally, 'my heart is not lifted up', i.e. 'I am not proud'.

neque elati sunt oculi Cf. Ps. 17.28, *Et oculos superborum humiliabis.*

Neque ambulavi in magnis Literally, 'nor have I walked among great things', i.e. 'lived in pursuit of them'. *Ambulare* in this sense is a Hebraism. Cf. *abire,* Ps. 1.1 and Ps. 118.1 ... *qui ambulant in lege Domini.*

in magnis ... mirabilibus super me 'among things too great ... too wonderful for me'. In imitation of Hebrew which lacks a comparative degree for the adjective, the positive degrees of *magnus* and *mirabilis* are used with *super* (literally, 'above') (= **min**, the Hebrew comparative particle).

130.2 **Si non humiliter sentiebam ... ita retributio** LXX and so V transform the positive tone of the Hebrew to a self-imposed curse: 'If I was not humbly minded, but exalted my soul, like a child weaned upon its mother, may there be retribution on my soul (= *me*).' In the Hebrew îm lo᾽ (*si non*) has asseverative function (= 'surely'). Cf. MT: 'Surely I have stilled and quieted my soul like one being weaned with its mother, like the one being weaned is my soul within me.' In part, the difference arose because LXX read gᵉmûl (= *retributio*) instead of a repeated gāmul ('weaned').

sed The Hebrew should have been rendered *et.*

exaltavi Translates exactly LXX ὕψωσα which in Hebrew would be rômamtî. The MT reads dômamtî ('I silenced') which is probably correct. The Hebrew consonants 'd' and 'r' are similar in form. Note Jer., *silere feci animam meam.*

sicut ablactatum super matrem suam 'like a child (sufficiently) weaned upon its mother'. Obviously not well connected in V and so variously emended and interpreted: e.g. Augustine's text reads: *quemadmodum qui ablatus est a lacte super matrem sic retributio in animam meam,* 'If I was not humbly minded but raised up my soul, so may retribution (fall upon) me (as upon) one who has been taken from the milk upon his mother' (or) 'as upon one who, being upon his mother, has been taken from the milk'. To him *mater* = 'the Church'. The text is obviously an attempted harmonization. A forced interpretation is the notion that a weaned child as a burden upon the mother is parallel to the burdensome retribution on the soul. Mothers were constrained to wean children at one time in the East up to the age of three.

130.3 **ex hoc nunc** 'henceforth' = LXX ἀπὸ τοῦ νῦν, *hoc* being used for the Greek definite article.

Psalm 132

The original setting of this Psalm is obscure. It may have been a wisdom Psalm extolling harmony in extended families; or it may have served a cultic purpose and was perhaps sung during the pilgrimage festivals to celebrate the assemblage of the covenant community in Jerusalem.

132.1 **Ecce quam bonum et quam iucundum habitare fratres in unum** To the Christian Augustine and others, a verse which divinely inspired the foundation of monastic communities.

habitare fratres In Hebrew the reference may be secular and allude to extended family situations; but the verb 'to dwell' may also refer to temple worship.

in unum 'together'. The Hebrew is slightly more emphatic, gam-yāḥad, 'also together', i.e. 'all-together'.

132.2 **Sicut** '(to dwell thus is) like ...'.

unguentum Hebrew 'the precious oil' used to consecrate the high priest. As the oil serves to dedicate the priest to God, so *habitare in unum* serves to dedicate His people to Himself.

Aaron Genitive case. The elder brother of Moses and first high priest of the Hebrews. Here the name is used generally for any priest. To Augustine, Aaron is a type of Christ who was at once Victim and Priest.

descendit Augustine interprets sequentially. The oil (Holy Spirit) descended from the Head (Christ) to the Beard (the Apostles) to the Garment (the Church and its monasteries).

barbam barbam The repetition, if original, may be intensifying or emphatic.

in ora vestimenti eius Some manuscripts have *in oram vestimenti eius*, 'to the edge of his garment'. Final *m*, often not pronounced in later Latin, may have dropped off. More likely *ora* is from *os*, an imitation of the Hebrew pî (= 'mouth' or 'edge'). Note common *os gladii* – 'the edge of the sword'. Also 1 Esdras 9.11 and *ab ore usque ad os*, 'from end to end'. The Hebrew may refer to the upper or lower hem of the garment. Hence the Revised Version translation 'to the collar of his vestment'. More probably the poet had in mind the deliberately pervasive image of the oil descending from the head to the feet.

132.3   Sicut ros Hermon qui descendit in montes Sion Hermon is a high mountain 200 miles north of Jerusalem. To solve the geographical difficulty, Jerome in Jer. read *montana Sion* instead of *montes Sion*, but Hermon is probably used here proverbially for a place of heavy dew. Augustine draws on its alleged Hebrew meaning 'a light set on a high place' to make it refer to Christ the source of grace (*ros*). *Sion* to him is the Church. For dew symbolizing a divine blessing, cf. 14.6, *ero quasi ros Israhel germinabit quasi lilium ... .*

Quoniam Hebrew kî here is probably emphatic, 'truly', rather than causal ('since').

illic The position of the adverb is emphatic. It may allude to a situation (*habitare fratres in unum*) or place (*Zion*).

vitam usque in saeculum May have referred originally only to perpetuation of the family line, but, to Augustine, the allusion is to eternal life in heaven.

Psalm 150

The Psalm, perhaps composed to end the whole Psalter, calls upon creation to praise God.

150.1   Alleluia An interjection of praise or joy which occurs 24 times in the Psalter. It transliterates Greek ἀλληλουϊά which in turn transliterates Hebrew **halluyah**, 'praise the Lord'. Following the practice of Origen, Jerome especially regarded Hebrew interjections as untranslatable. Psalms 145-150 form a collection of Psalms of praise marked by this recurring interjection.

Laudate In Hebrew, the same verbal root occurs as in **halluyah**, but in V it is now translated *laudate* ten times.

in sanctis eius The Latin allows two interpretations: (1) *sanctis* is a Hebraizing neuter plural of intensity from *sancta*, 'the most Holy Place, the temple', whether the earthly or heavenly sanctuary; (2)

sanctis is masculine plural, 'in (or because of) His pious persons'; 'saints' to Augustine. Hebrew parallelism (here to *firmamentum*) suggests interpretation 1.

    in firmamento virtutis eius *Firmamentum* refers to the vault of heaven which separates the waters above from the waters below. The phrase literally reproduces the Hebrew construct chain: 'in the firmament of His power', which may mean either (1) 'in His mighty firmament' or (2) 'in the firmament that manifests His power'. In Hebrew the pronominal suffix is placed at the end of a construct chain but normally is to be translated with the whole chain.

150.2   **in virtutibus eius** Here, 'for His acts of power', but cf. *Dominus virtutum*, 'Lord of hosts'. The abstract noun is used in the plural in a concrete sense. Again, *in = propter*.

    secundum multitudinem magnitudinis eius Literally, 'by reason of the multitude of His power', i.e. 'for the greatness of His power'. The too literal imitation of Hebrew leads Augustine to interpret *multitudinem* concretely as a reference to God's saints.

150.3   **in sono tubae** The preposition expresses means: 'with the sound of the horn', a signalling instrument whether in battle or at festivals, hence appropriately mentioned first. Unlike a Latin *tuba*, the šôpār was curved; thus Jerome's later correction to *bucinae* in Jer.

    psalterio A type of stringed instrument, a lyre with a slanting yoke.

    cithara 'a lyre' with a sounding box.

150.4   **tympano** 'tambourine' or 'hand drum'.

    choro 'dance' or 'choir'.

    cordis 'stringed instruments'.

    organo 'organ pipe'; in Hebrew, a straight flute.

150.5   **in cymbalis iubilationis** Literally, 'with the cymbals of shouting', i.e. 'with the noisy cymbals', larger perhaps and louder than the *cymbala bene sonantia*. In later Christian thought, various underlying meanings were attached to the different instruments: e.g. the *tympana*, being made of dead beasts' hides, teach mortification of the flesh; the strings under great tension and strain are types of those who fast and keep vigils. To Augustine, the musical references include voice, breath, and striking which here represent mind, spirit and body.

150.6 omnis spiritus The meaning is clearer in Jer., *omne quod spirat*, 'everything that breathes'. Augustine interprets spiritually: *et quia sapere secundum carnem mors est, omnis spiritus laudet Dominum.*